The

Death

of

Outrage

*Bill Clinton and
the Assault on
American Ideals*

William J. Bennett

A TOUCHSTONE BOOK

Published by Simon & Schuster

邢

TOUCHSTONE
Rockefeller Center
1230 Avenue of the Americas
New York, NY 10020

First Touchstone Edition 1999

Designed by Pei Loi Koay

Manufactured in the United States of America

10 9 8 7 6 5 4 3 2 1

Library of Congress Cataloging-in-Publication Data
Bennett, William J. (William John)
      The death of outrage: Bill Clinton and the assault on American
ideals/ William J. Bennett.
          p.   cm.
          1. Clinton, Bill, 1946–   —Ethics.   2. United States—Politics
and government—1993–   —Moral and ethical aspects.   3. Clinton,
Bill, 1946–   —Sexual behavior.   4. Political corruption—United
States—History—20th century.   I. Title.
    E886.2.B47   1998
    973.929'092—dc21   98-36055
                                                                                    CIP

ISBN: 0-684-81372-6
ISBN: 0-684-86403-7 (Pbk)

Contents

Introduction   1

Chapter 1   Sex   13

Chapter 2   Character   31

Chapter 3   Politics   53

Chapter 4   Ken Starr   73

Chapter 5   Law   93

Chapter 6   Judgment   111

Conclusion   127

Afterword   135

Afterword to the
New Edition   136

Appendix: 156
*The Nixon and Clinton
Administration Scandals:
A Comparison*

OTHER BOOKS BY WILLIAM J. BENNETT

Our Sacred Honor

Body Count

The Children's Book of Virtues

The Moral Compass

The Book of Virtues

The Index of Leading Cultural Indicators

The Devaluing of America

Introduction

It is a fairly well known fact, I suppose, that I am a public critic of President Clinton. What is less well known is that it has not always been thus.

During the 1980s, although we had deep and substantial political disagreements on many issues, I had good things to say about Bill Clinton. When I was secretary of education and he was governor of Arkansas, I was impressed with his work on education, and publicly praised him. I considered him (along with Lamar Alexander of Tennessee, Bob Graham of Florida, and Tom Kean of New Jersey) to be among the nation's top education reform governors. I appointed his wife, Hillary, to an education commission. In those days he was chairman of the Democratic Leadership Council, a centrist group within the Democratic party and one with which I have often been in sympathy. As a standard-bearer of the national Democratic party, he seemed to me much more responsible on public policy issues than either George McGovern or Michael Dukakis, the Democratic presidential nominees in 1972 and

1988, respectively. I said as much during a 1988 exchange with Governor Clinton on *The MacNeil-Lehrer News Hour.*

Early in his presidential administration we corresponded, and once in a while he had kind public words to say about me. Through the years I have thought him remarkably talented and affable, charming, and engaging. He possesses a sharp, inquiring mind. And in terms of sheer political ability—retail politics—I consider him among the best talents this nation has seen.

But I have changed my opinion of Bill Clinton, dramatically so, because of the mounting evidence of deep corruption. We see this in the attempts to delay and derail criminal and congressional investigations. In the avalanche of lies. In the tactics of intimidation. In the misuse of office. And in the abuse of power.

For me, things crystallized on these matters on Wednesday morning, January 21, 1998, with this *Washington Post* headline:

"Clinton Accused of Urging Aide to Lie"

The article reported that on the previous Friday three federal judges, sitting as an appeals court panel and acting at the request and with the approval of the attorney general of the United States, had authorized independent counsel Kenneth W. Starr to expand an already-existing investigation in order to examine allegations of suborning perjury, making false statements under oath, and obstruction of justice. Each criminal allegation directly involved the president of the United States. As we all know, at the center of the scandal was Monica Lewinsky, who began work as a White House intern in 1995, when she was twenty-one. And so a story came to light that now dominates the American political landscape.

The nation's initial reaction to the story was shock and surprise. Upon reflection, however, it is clear that there was very little shocking or unexpected about it. Because the story revealed the essence of Bill Clinton. It was a perfect snapshot.

A quarter-century ago, a "third-rate burglary" and the crimes that followed it consumed and eventually devoured the second-term presidency of Richard Milhous Nixon. Today we see how a tawdry sexual affair with an intern, and the acts that followed it, have consumed—though they have not yet devoured—the second-term presidency of William Jefferson Clinton.

The Lewinsky scandal represents more, much more, than reckless sexual misconduct. It now involves very public, very emphatic lies. Breaches of trust. The subversion of truth. The possibility of criminal wrongdoing. And so we face the identical question today that we faced a generation ago: is this president—is *any* president—above the law? Despite the best efforts of Bill Clinton and his people, the salaciousness surrounding the scandal ultimately cannot obscure the more profound underlying issue: violations of law and efforts to undermine constitutional government.

And on these matters, the evidence and the facts lead overwhelmingly to one conclusion: Bill Clinton committed a crime when he lied under oath about his sexual affair, in the Oval Office, with a twenty-one-year-old intern. It is worth noting that former and current Clinton advisers and many other Democrats* agree. The affair and the cover-up are now inextricably intertwined. It is now a conditional

---

*Wall Street Journal columnist Al Hunt wrote in late February: "Mr. Clinton's predicament was evident at several recent dinner parties and interviews. No one believed the president's explanation about his relationship with former intern Monica Lewinsky; terms like disgraceful, reckless and contemptible were tossed about—all by prominent Democratic office holders and high-level Clinton appointees." In talking about President Clinton's relationship with Monica Lewinsky, the president's own top spokesman, Michael McCurry, admitted to the *Chicago Tribune*, "Maybe there'll be a simple, innocent explanation. I don't think so, because I think we would have offered that up already. . . . I think it's going to end up being a very complicated story. . . . And I don't think it's going to be entirely easy to explain." And during a discussion with former Clinton adviser David Gergen, *Newsweek*'s Michael Isikoff said that when the Lewinsky story first broke, senior White House aides were wondering not only whether the president would resign, but whether he *should* resign.

proposition: *if* the president had a sexual relationship with Monica Lewinsky, *then* he lied under oath. It appears that lies have begotten more lies and that perjury has begotten obstruction of justice.

I come to these conclusions because of the overwhelming weight of the reported, and so far unrebutted, evidence, including the now-familiar litany: twenty hours of tapes, thirty-seven White House visits by Miss Lewinsky after she was no longer an intern, gifts, job placement help from Vernon Jordan, a job offer from then–U.N. Ambassador Bill Richardson, the president's initial, unconvincing denial, and much more. Because, given Bill Clinton's past pattern of behavior, this story is so likely true.* Because the president is acting like a man who has done wrong. Because for so long he refused to answer in detail any of the important questions. Because we are correct to draw reasonable inferences from the president's six-and-a-half-month de facto invocation of his Fifth Amendment right against self-incrimination.

The president at last agreed to speak. After refusing a reported half-dozen invitations to address the grand jury voluntarily, on July 17 he was served with a subpoena *compelling* him to testify. With few legal and political options now left open to him, the president finally, reluctantly, said he would address the criminal allegations against him. But in typical Clinton fashion the White House insisted that the subpoena be withdrawn after the deal was agreed to, so President Clinton could say he was testifying "voluntarily"— even though, of course, there would have been no testimony without the pressure of a subpoena.

I have asked repeatedly since the scandal broke: if the president had nothing to hide, why did he hide? Common sense is helpful here. A person innocent of what the president is accused of doing would be shouting his innocence from the rooftop. He would not wait for a subpoena to finally declare himself on these matters. Nor would

---

*"The problem is that what we're hearing sounds true, it smells true," one White House aide told a reporter.

he pass up any opportunity to embarrass his critics by quickly establishing his innocence beyond dispute, and in so doing force from his critics retractions, apologies, mea culpas. But the president can do none of this. After promising in January to say "more rather than less, sooner rather than later," in late April he declared he is "absolutely" prepared to leave allegations of criminal conduct hanging for the rest of his presidency. A reasonable person can only assume that he did not willingly answer in detail the questions posed to him because he knows the truth will harm him.

In the seven months since the story first broke, we have gradually seen illusions give way to reality, as finally they must. What have been revealed, through this scandal and others, are the worst elements of Bill Clinton's private *and* public character: reckless and irresponsible private behavior; habitual lying; abuse of power. Bill Clinton is a reproach. He has defiled the office of the presidency of the United States.

These are harsh words about our president. They are also reluctant words. No responsible citizen can easily make such claims about his president. But they are considered words. For this president—who famously promised us "the most ethical administration in the history of the republic"—must be considered among the most corrupt in the history of the republic. Corruption in office matters. And corruption in the highest office in the land matters a lot.

It has been said—correctly, in my estimation—that the crimes of Watergate were not an aberration; they were instead the inevitable result of a particular political culture fostered and nurtured by the Nixon administration. A similar claim can be made about the Lewinsky scandal. Skulduggery, half-truths, stonewalling, breaches of ethics, and even contempt for the law have characterized the Clinton presidency. Consider:

- The improper acquisition of hundreds of FBI files on political adversaries.

- The mysterious reappearance (in the Clintons' private living quarters) of subpoenaed billing records crucial to a Federal Deposit Insurance Corporation investigation that had been purportedly missing for two years.

- Billing records through which the inspector general of the FDIC found that Hillary Clinton had prepared documents used "to deceive federal bank examiners" in their investigation of Madison Guarantee Savings & Loan.

- Payments by Clinton friends and associates of upward of $700,000 to Webster Hubbell, the former associate attorney general and one of the president's closest friends, after he was forced to resign in disgrace and at a time when Hubbell was being asked to provide evidence of presidential wrongdoing to the independent counsel. The payments—some arranged by Vernon Jordan—coincided with Mr. Hubbell's refusal to help investigators looking into wrongdoing by the president and the first lady (after Mr. Hubbell had initially agreed to assist prosecutors).

- The crass and unprecedented selling of the Lincoln bedroom to raise reelection money.

- Improper fund-raising calls made from the White House.

- The president's statement to donors, captured on videotape, that he was raising soft money to pay for ads that aided his reelection (an act that may well be illegal and a statement that was contrary to his previous denials).

- The White House's failure to turn over to congressional investigators videotapes of Mr. Clinton's coffees with political donors until months after they were requested.

- Scores of potential witnesses who either fled the country or invoked the Fifth Amendment during congressional investigations into possible illegal fundraising by the DNC and the Clinton-Gore re-election campaign—including a number of the key figures who were associates of the president. FBI director Louis Freeh said the only time he faced similar obstacles to an investigation was in prosecuting organized crime in New York.

. The failure to turn over subpoenaed notes by White House aide Bruce Lindsey until the day after the Senate White-water Committee's authorization expired.

. The fact that when Paula Jones's lawyers subpoenaed letters from Kathleen Willey, Mr. Clinton falsely denied that he had any such documents—but two months later, after Ms. Willey went public on *60 Minutes* with her allegations of presidential groping, Mr. Clinton personally approved the release of fifteen notes and letters in an effort to discredit her.

. President Clinton's initial claim through his lawyer that he had "no specific recollection" of a meeting with Ms. Willey. But during his deposition in the Paula Jones civil case, the president said he has "a very clear memory" of the meeting.

. The improper use of the FBI to bolster false White House claims of financial malfeasance in the firing of the White House Travel Office.

. The admission of the Pentagon's chief spokesman, Assistant Defense Secretary Kenneth Bacon, to orchestrating the release of the personnel information of Linda Tripp, a violation of the Privacy Act.

. The efforts to obstruct the Resolution Trust Corporation's investigation of the failed Arkansas thrift, Madison Guaranty Savings & Loan, which was involved in a sham real estate venture.*

---

*RTC investigator Jean Lewis said there was a "concerted effort to obstruct, hamper, and manipulate" the Madison investigation; former deputy treasury secretary Roger Altman briefed top White House aides on the procedures the RTC was following in a possible civil case against Madison Guaranty; and Mr. Altman was under "intense pressure" from the White House not to recuse himself from the case.

• The administration's misrepresentation about Mrs. Clinton's suspicious 1978–79 investments in cattle futures, in which she made $100,000 on $1,000. At first the White House said Mrs. Clinton did the trades herself and got out of this "nerve-wracking" game when she was pregnant; when that story proved false, the White House revealed that most of the trades were in fact placed by Clinton friend and Tyson Foods lawyer James Blair.

To put it in a broader perspective consider this simple fact: if the president is innocent of the various allegations made against him, a large number of people, representing all points on the political spectrum, have committed perjury.

By his actions, then, we are witnessing an assault on American ideals.

Bill Clinton is completing the second year of his second term. Why not let these matters go? Instead of keeping the nation's attention focused on scandals and squalid acts, why not move on to other issues? Why not just look away?

The answer to these questions is that on Bill Clinton's behalf, in his defense, many bad ideas are being put into widespread circulation. It is said that private character has virtually no impact on governing character; that what matters above all is a healthy economy; that moral authority is defined solely by how well a president deals with public policy matters; that America needs to become more European (read: more "sophisticated") in its attitude toward sex; that lies about sex, even under oath, don't really matter; that we shouldn't be "judgmental"; that it is inappropriate to make preliminary judgments about the president's conduct because he hasn't been found guilty in a court of law; and so forth.

If these arguments take root in American soil—if they become the coin of the public realm—we will have validated them, and we will come to rue the day we did. These arguments define us down; they assume a lower common denominator of behavior and leadership than we Americans ought to accept. And if we do accept it, we will have committed an unthinking act of moral and intellectual disarmament. In the realm of American ideals and the great tradition of public debate, the high ground will have been lost. And when we need to rely again on this high ground—as surely we will need to—we will find it drained of its compelling moral power. In that sense, then, the arguments invoked by Bill Clinton and his defenders represent an assault on American ideals, even if you assume the president did nothing improper. So the arguments need to be challenged.

I believe these arguments are also a threat to our understanding of American self-government. It demands active participation in, and finally, reasoned judgments on, important civic matters. "Judgment" is a word that is out of favor these days, but it remains a cornerstone of democratic self-government. It is what enables us to hold ourselves, and our leaders, to high standards. It is how we distinguish between right and wrong, noble and base, honor and dishonor. We cannot ignore that responsibility, or foist it on others. It is the price—sometimes the exacting price—of citizenship in a democracy. The most popular arguments made by the president's supporters invite us to abandon that participation, those standards, and the practice of making those distinctions.

Bill Clinton's presidency is also defining *public* morality down. Civilized society must give public affirmation to principles and standards, categorical norms, notions of right and wrong. Even though public figures often fall short of these standards—and we know and we expect some will—it is nevertheless crucial that we pay tribute to them. When Senator Gary Hart withdrew from the 1988 presidential contest because of his relationship with Donna Rice, he told his staff, "Through thoughtlessness and misjudgment I've let each of you down. And I deeply regret that." By saying what he said, by withdrawing from the race, Senator Hart *affirmed* public standards. President Clinton, by contrast, expresses no regret, no remorse, no contrition—even as he uses his public office to further his private ends. On every scandal, what he says or intimates always amounts to one of the following: "It doesn't matter. I wasn't involved. My political enemies are to blame. I have nothing more to say. The rules don't apply to me. There are no consequences to my actions. It's irrelevant. My only responsibility is to do the people's business." This is moral bankruptcy, and it is damaging our country, its standards, and our self-respect.

Once in a great while a single national event provides insight into where we are and who we are and what we esteem. The Clinton presidency has provided us with a window onto our times, our moral order, our understanding of citizenship. The many Clinton scandals tell us, in a way few other events can, where we are in our public philosophy. They reveal insights into how we view politics and power; virtue and vice; public trust and respect for the law; sexual morality and standards of personal conduct.

America's professional opinion classes—journalists, columnists, and commentators—have produced truckloads of words, both spoken and written, about the Clinton scandals. Some of them are excellent, and I have mined them for this book. What I hope to do is to put things in a broader context, explaining their implications for our national political life and for the lessons we teach our young.

My goal is also to give public expression to people's private concerns. Many Americans have an intuitive understanding that something is deeply troubling about President Clinton's conduct and the defenses offered on his behalf. But Bill Clinton and his supporters have skillfully deflected criticism by changing the subject. They have persuaded many in the middle that the sophisticated thing is to dismiss the scandalous as irrelevant. My purpose in this book is to speak citizen to citizen to those in the middle—not to "preach to the converted," but to speak to the troubled. I believe that public opinion has not yet hardened on these matters and that people are still open to evidence, facts, persuasion, and an appeal to reason and the rule of law. This book is presented in that spirit.

This is a short book. It is not a systematic work of moral philosophy. Its aim is much more limited: to respond to an urgent public matter now before the American people—in a manner, I trust, that is informed by sound reasoning. In what follows I take the words of the president and his defenders seriously, examining them, and asking the reader to judge whether the conclusions that flow from them are true or false, good or harmful.

In the end this book rests on the venerable idea that moral good and moral harm are very real things, and moral good or moral harm can come to a society by what it esteems and by what it disdains.

Many people have been persuaded to take a benign view of the Clinton presidency on the basis of arguments that have attained an almost talismanic stature but that in my judgment are deeply wrong and deeply pernicious. We need to say no to those arguments as loudly as we can—and yes to the American ideals they endanger.

Chapter 1

Sex

Defense of President Clinton: *One of the most often invoked defenses of President Clinton is that this case is only about sex. In the words of CNN's* Crossfire *co-host Bill Press, "With . . . one admission, Monica Lewinsky exposes the total absurdity of the entire Starr investigation: it's about sex." From there, the argument becomes: a president's private sexual behavior is none of the people's business.*

Geraldo Rivera, host of a CNBC program, says he is "sure something probably happened" between Bill Clinton and Monica Lewinsky, but even if the president has done everything he is accused of, at worst "he's a hypocrite. So what? Get over it." Washington Post *columnist Mary McGrory writes of "the simple truth that has been apparent to the man and the woman in the street from day one: reprehensible is not impeachable. Americans would prefer a monogamous husband. But . . . they are not going to insist on it. Monkey business in the Oval Office just doesn't make the constitutional standard of 'high crimes and mis-demeanors.'"* And feminist commentator Susan Estrich, the campaign manager for 1988 Democratic presidential nominee Michael Dukakis, asks, "Should allegedly finding comfort, release, satisfaction, peace in the arms of a beautiful twenty-one-year-old count for more than balancing the budget?"

The constant refrain is, "If the president's wife forgives him, why shouldn't we?" Feminist author Wendy Kaminer put it this way: "Why should we hold the president to standards of moral behavior that few of us meet consistently? . . . I'm not suggesting that the president's lies and infidelities don't matter. They must matter a lot to Hillary and Chelsea Clinton. But why should they matter to voters?" A Republican entrepreneur in Naperville, Illinois, told the Washington Post, "If he harassed Paula Jones, well, that would be a bad thing, but that's for the two of them to work out. Likewise, if he slept with Monica Lewinsky, that's for the two of them and Hillary to work through. I don't think any of that is among the more pressing issues of the day for the American people."

These beliefs give rise to the conviction that because adultery is none of our business, the Starr investigation into the Lewinsky matter has been illegitimate from the get-go. The real scandal is the Starr investigation's zealous, thinly disguised moral crusade. Former South Dakota Senator George McGovern, the Democrats' 1972 presidential nominee, refers to Judge Starr as "prosecutor-at-large of presidential sex," and says he has come to one conclusion: "Even if Bill Clinton has yielded to an occasional attack of lust and is too embarrassed to tell us all about it, those sins have done far less damage to the American public and our democracy than is being done by a federal prosecutor rampaging across the land year after year."

Others argue that there are lies—and then there are LIES. In this context, there are some things—i.e., sexual matters—we should *lie* about. To the National Journal's Jonathan Rauch, a *thoughtful observer, "the one sort of lie that a civilized culture not only condones but depends upon [is] a consensual lie about consensual adultery. . . . The only way to insist that adultery is intolerable while actually tolerating it is by hiding it in the closet." While conceding that the president of the United States should obey the law and not cheat with interns, Rauch implores us to understand "this is the real world, not The Sound of Music." Michael J. Sandel, a professor of government at Harvard, writes that "there may be a case, in the name of privacy and decorum, for the president to deny a scurrilous charge even if true, provided it has no bearing on public responsibilities." And Hendrik Hertzberg of The New Yorker says we should distinguish between "pernicious falsehoods calculated to cover up crimes against humanity and, say, feeble fibs aimed at wiggling out of some horribly embarrassing and essentially victimless but legal piece of human stupidity."*

Clinton supporters argue that the public's apparent indifference to the Clinton scandals, as supported by the polls, is a sign that we are becoming more tolerant and grounded—a sophisticated sensibility long ago achieved by Europeans. Actor and sometimes political adviser Warren Beatty put it this way: "Maybe America is becoming less reluctant to sweep it [sex] under the rug, more accepting of its own sexual difficulties. America is becoming more like the countries that America came from." In other words, the ho-hum reaction to possible presidential misconduct reflects a wiser understanding of human nature and the ways of the world, a welcome liberation.

Response

The core of this argument is that independent counsel Kenneth Starr's investigation is merely about sex, and sexual misconduct is none of our business—even if it involves a married president and a young intern—because it is victimless and tells us nothing of relevance. If sexual sins were considered disqualifying, many good past presidents would not have served in office—and of course privacy and civilized culture demand that we lie about sex. The Starr investigation itself is nothing but an anti-sex crusade, and America should be less uptight and more sophisticated and European about sexual matters. I will respond to each of these claims.

I

The notion that President Clinton's sexual activity is the object of the investigation by the independent counsel is false. At the heart of the Lewinsky scandal is Attorney General Reno's finding that there exists credible evidence of *criminal* wrongdoing by the president of the United States. The independent counsel did not decide arbitrarily to rummage around the president's sex life and then happen to come across possible wrongdoing, as some suggest. It is not, as lawyer Gerry Spence argues, a "panty raid." Serious allegations of perjury, obstruction of justice, and job offers for silence—not accusations of presidential philandering—were the investigation's trip wire.

Whenever possible, however, the president's defenders turn the focus away from criminal conspiracy and toward matters of sex. This is a dishonest, though not unintelligent, strategy. Apologists for the president are attempting to tap into a new attitude in the country toward sexual relations, one that has been deeply influenced by the sexual revolution. The manifestation of this "live-and-let-live" sentiment can be seen vividly today, when it is widely asserted that sexual relations between consenting adults—even when they involve a married president's relationship with a young White House intern—are a personal matter that we ought not judge whatever the context. The strategy is to render this a debate about "purely private sexual behavior," and, once that beachhead is established, to portray the president's critics as intolerant Puritans.

Listen to the typically measured words of presidential adviser James Carville: "These people [the office of independent counsel] are obsessed with sex. This thing is totally out of control. . . . He's [Ken Starr] a sex-obsessed person who's out to get the president. . . . He's concerned about three things: sex, sex, and more sex. That's all that man's about. . . . It's about sex." And Carville mocks Judge Starr because Starr let it be known he is a Christian who sings hymns on morning walks along the Potomac River. "He plants a story, he goes down by the Potomac and listens to hymns, as the cleansing waters of the Potomac go by, and we are going to wash all the Sodomites and fornicators out of town."

All the president's men do this because they know this is their most fertile ground; they must attempt relentlessly to portray their opposition as bigoted and intolerant fanatics who have no respect for privacy. At the same time they offer a temptation to their supporters: the temptation to see themselves as realists, worldly-wise, sophisticated: in a word, European.

That temptation should be resisted by the rest of us. In America, morality is central to our politics and attitudes in a way that is not the case in Europe, and precisely this moral streak is what is best about us. It is a moral streak that has made America uncommonly generous in its dealings with foreign nations (in matters ranging from the Marshall Plan, to the sending of peacekeeping troops, to disaster relief, to much else); liberated Europe from the Nazi threat and the Iron Curtain; and prevented noxious political movements like fascism from taking root at home. Europeans may have some things to teach us about, say, wine or haute couture. But on the matter of morality in politics, America has much to teach Europe.

In this chapter I am going to take the bait offered by James Carville, and speak for those allegedly intolerant Puritans who have the effrontery to believe that a president's sex life is, or can be, a matter of public consequence.

II

In much of modern America, there seems to be a belief that anything that involves sex is, or ought to be, forgotten; here we see a River Lethe effect permeating our culture. In Greek mythology, Lethe is one of the rivers of Hades. The souls of the dead are obliged to taste its water, so that they may forget everything said and done while alive. Today, many Americans feel we should drink the water and forget. The sentiment is one should simply respond to sexual misconduct with that watchword of our time, "Whatever." Sex becomes a No Accountability Zone. However, "what's at stake in the Lewinsky scandal is not the right to privacy," conservative writer David Frum has pointed out correctly, "but the central dogma of the baby boomers: the belief that sex, so long as it's consensual, ought never to be subject to moral scrutiny at all."

But that posture does not withstand scrutiny; upon close examination, it is finally indefensible. What we need are commonsensical and principled standards in order to decide which private behaviors are subject to moral scrutiny, and which are not.

The right to be left alone about sexual matters is an admirable American sentiment. Sex is the most intimate of all human acts; it is fraught with mystery, passion, vulnerability. On this issue more than any other, we rightly insist on a large zone of privacy. Nobody wants state-sponsored voyeurism.

Throughout history, however, most societies have known that sex is a quintessentially moral activity, and they cannot therefore be completely indifferent toward it. Societies have long recognized that sex affects us at the deepest level of our being. As John Donne wrote, "Love's mysteries in souls do grow." And here is President Clinton's favorite, Walt Whitman, in *Leaves of Grass:*

Sex contains all,
Bodies, Souls, meanings, proofs, purities, delicacies, results,
   promulgations,
Songs, commands, health, pride, the maternal mystery, the
   seminal milk;
All hopes, benefactions, bestowals,
All the passions, loves, beauties, delights of the earth,
All the governments, judges, gods, follow'd persons of the
   earth,
These are contain'd in sex as parts of itself and justifications
   of itself.

Poets and philosophers, saints and psychiatrists have known that the power and beauty of sex lie precisely in the fact that it is not just something you like to do or don't like to do. Far from being value-neutral, sex may be the most value-laden of any human activity. It does no good to try to sanitize or deny or ignore this truth. The act of sex has complicated and profound repercussions. To deny this, to consider it to be something less special and powerful than it is, is a dodge and a lie.

Sexual indiscipline can be a threat to the stability of crucial human affairs. That is one reason why we seek to put it under ritual and marriage vow. In the military, for instance, sex between superior officers and underlings is destructive not only of order, but of the principle of merit that underlies our presumptions about why rewards and punishments are meted out. Acts of infidelity in the military or in the workplace can result in special treatment being accorded to some individuals rather than others, lead to jealousies and competitions that are disorderly, introduce irrationality into the process of decision-making, and render individuals vulnerable to blackmail or bribery. And when a sexual affair ends, passions may be present that are destructive to both parties.

Much, perhaps most, of the public commentary about President Clinton's adulterous relationships makes them seem unimportant, trivial, of no real concern. Sex is reduced to a mere riot of the glands. Susan Estrich, for example, breezily excuses the president's adultery ("finding comfort . . . in the arms of a beautiful twenty-one-year-old") in a way that one assumes she would not excuse in her husband. Hendrik Hertzberg considers it stupid to get caught but not wrong to commit adultery, an "essentially victimless" activity. An aggrieved spouse might take exception to that characterization; even Bill Clinton admitted to—note the words carefully—"causing pain" in his marriage.

In extramarital affairs, there *are* victims. In marriage, one person has been entrusted with the soul of another. That power, freely given, is unlike any other human relationship; so, too, is the damage that can be done. This ought not to be made light of, shrugged off, made fun of.

It is culturally telling that the president's adulterous relationships elicit yawns, while Linda Tripp's secretly recorded phone conversations of Monica Lewinsky elicit rage. Geraldo Rivera urges us to "get over it" when the issue is the president's betrayal of his wife, but because she has "decided to betray her young friend," Linda Tripp is guilty of a "violation . . . of ethics, decency, and loyalty"; she is "treacherous, back-stabbing, good-for-nothing." This despite the apparent fact that Ms. Tripp was pressured by Ms. Lewinsky to lie under oath; her truthfulness was challenged after Tripp said she saw Kathleen Willey leave the Oval Office after Ms. Willey fended off (according to Willey) unwanted sexual advances by the president; and Tripp knew this White House has made a habit of destroying the reputation of women who might implicate Mr. Clinton in wrongdoing. A fair-minded person might disavow what Linda Tripp did even while conceding that there were compelling reasons that would justify her actions. What similar justification is there for adultery?

But assume for the sake of the argument that there were no extenuating circumstances to help explain why Ms. Tripp did what she did. Assume it was the betrayal of a friend. Why all the venom directed at Ms. Tripp, and at the same time justification for the president? Why are people so quick to censure Tripp's actions, and so willing to excuse the president's? Why would the secret taping of a co-worker be considered magnitudes worse than the betrayal of a spouse?

It is time to acknowledge in public what we know to be true in private: adultery is a betrayal of a very high order, the betrayal of a person one has promised to honor. It often shatters fragile, immensely important social networks (made up of spouses, children, extended family, and mutual friends). It violates a solemn vow. When it is discovered, acute emotional damage almost always follows, often including the damage of divorce.

One reason society needs to uphold high public standards in this realm is because sex—when engaged in capriciously, without restraint, and against those in positions of relative weakness—can be exploitive and harmful. Civilizations understand that we need to construct social guardrails to protect the vulnerable against the rapacious. And these social guardrails are not simply the products of the law; they are built as well by moral codes. Leaders who flout moral codes weaken them.

There is a broader point to be made as well. While high standards and good conduct are reinforced by just laws, a crucial role is played by public sentiment. It is axiomatic that social mores are shaped by public approbation and disapprobation. So we should ask: are we better off with a public ethic that is indifferent toward adultery?

Some (like the writer Jonathan Rauch) are in favor of a public ethic that condemns adultery but that also permits us to lie about it. Rauch's reasoning is that if we begin "outing" adulterers, we will no longer be able to stigmatize adultery itself because the act is just "too common." And so, instead of changing adulterous behavior, we will end up causing people to become indifferent to it. Adultery will therefore be excused morally. Or so the argument goes.

First, an important empirical point. Adultery is not nearly so common as Mr. Rauch and many others think. The most comprehensive study of American sexual patterns comes from the National Opinion Research Center at the University of Chicago. According to the NORC survey, 21 percent of men and 11 percent of women have committed adultery at some point in their married lives. Within the previous twelve months, 3.6 percent of men and only 1.3 percent of women reported an infidelity. And the data suggest that only a small percentage of those who commit adultery are serial adulterers.

Second, Rauch says we should "wink" and lie about consensual adultery and, in effect, do all we can to keep adulterous affairs quiet—for "civilized culture not only condones but depends upon" keeping such things quiet. Notice, however, that Rauch ignores the logic of his own argument. Rather than helping the president keep his "consensual lies" quiet, Rauch declares very bluntly, very openly, very publicly that "it is beginning to look approximately 99.87 percent certain that Bill Clinton has done bad things." Why doesn't he keep quiet about Bill Clinton's "bad things"? In the end, Rauch asks of his readers what he cannot demand of himself: moral, civic, and legal blindness. (Leave aside the fact that, as I have already noted, this investigation is not driven by consensual lies or adultery but by questions of criminal cover-up and obstruction of justice.)

And even if it does serve a common social good to keep adultery "in the closet," that still doesn't provide guidance on how to deal with the situation President Clinton has presented us: namely, how to react when a sexual affair is *forced* in our face, on the front page, by the president's own irresponsible, self-indulgent conduct?

Once that occurs, what collectively do we have to say about it? Do we serve the cause of marital fidelity by winking at publicly known acts of a leader's adultery? Surely not. Yet that is exactly the situation in which we now find ourselves.

Women above all will reap the consequences of this squalid national drama, one of whose ironies is the rock-solid support for President Clinton shown by the feminist movement. In the wake of Kathleen Willey's testimony under oath that she had been groped in the White House by President Clinton, Gloria Steinem, the founder of *Ms.* magazine and perhaps America's most prominent feminist, took to the op-ed page of the *New York Times*.

According to Ms. Steinem: "The truth is that even if the allegations are true, the President is not guilty of sexual harassment. He is accused of having made a gross, dumb, and reckless pass at a supporter during a low point in her life. She pushed him away, she said, and it never happened again. In other words, President Clinton took 'no' for an answer."

Is *this* what the feminist movement has come to? To make the world safe for gropers and fondlers? To make socially acceptable a "no harm, no foul" rule? To give a green light to the sexual predator, so long as he stops short of rape and eventually takes no for an answer? To countenance the advances of a man in a powerful position who is ready and willing to take advantage of a woman? And to applaud Hillary Clinton, the wife of a chronically unfaithful husband, for standing by her man? These are the real-world signals being sent and, as night follows day, these are the real-world signals being received, by aggressive young men and vulnerable young women across America.

III

Many Clinton supporters contend that before we measure Bill Clinton's score on the adultery meter, we should first consider other presidents who might be disqualified on similar grounds. Franklin Roosevelt. John F. Kennedy. Lyndon Johnson. Warren Harding. Probably Thomas Jefferson. Maybe Dwight Eisenhower. Maybe others. Brown University Professor James Morone writes that fourteen out of forty-one presidents "set off whispers" of infidelity, and television pundit (and zealous Clinton defender) Eleanor Clift assures us that "libido and leadership" are linked.

Let's agree that adultery ought not automatically disqualify a person from seeking high public office. But let's agree, too, that at some point adultery will often reveal to us something important about a person's (and a president's) character and judgment; his prudence and judiciousness; his honor and trustworthiness; his governing ability and stability.

This is another point with which even Bill Clinton agrees. In *First in His Class,* David Marannis tells about a conversation between then-Governor Clinton and Betsey Wright, his chief of staff. The subject was Gary Hart's relationship with Donna Rice. According to the long-loyal Wright, Clinton "wanted to believe and advocated that it was irrelevant to whether the guy could be a good president." Betsey Wright, by contrast, argued that in the Hart case it was significant, because it raised questions about his stability; any previous affairs might have been irrelevant, but "to have one while he was running was foolhardy." According to Maraniss, "Clinton agreed. Hart, he said, was foolish to flaunt it."

Adultery is wrong. Still, reasonable distinctions can be made. Context and facts can matter. For example: it would matter whether a president had a discreet, isolated, long-ago affair, or whether he were a serial (and still-practicing) adulterer. It would matter if a president had been put on notice—if he knew his personal life would be under intense scrutiny—and still decided to run the risk and indulge in an affair, in the Oval Office, with young staffers. It would matter if there were an element of exploitation based on age and status. It would matter if the president used his public office to assist in, and cover up, his private fling(s). It would matter if the president acted sexually more like an alley cat than an adult—just as, conversely, it would matter if, after an affair, there was genuine contrition, a change of heart, a change of ways.

Of presidents and adultery, Professor Jean Bethke Elshtain of the University of Chicago has written masterfully: "Alas, we seem to have lost the ability to make coherent distinctions in this area. We say, 'Everybody does it.' But not every president had staffs assigned to 'bimbo eruptions.' Not every president had a 'nuts and sluts' detail. This is a pattern of behavior quite different from Franklin Roosevelt's affair with Lucy Mercer. . . . That an ill and lonely Roosevelt renewed the relationship as a friendship during his last years in office is light years removed from a public official deploying a small army of enablers or fixers when his 'private' behavior spins out of control. If Dwight Eisenhower had had an affair when he was supreme commander in Europe (and his family vehemently denies he did), well before he became president, that would scarcely have been the same thing as carrying on sexual dalliances . . . in one's office and then having staff risk legal trouble to cover them up."

Bill Clinton is unlike almost any other president in this regard, save perhaps his boyhood idol, John Kennedy. But President Kennedy was not an exception to the rule; in many ways he proves the rule. If President Kennedy had an affair with a mobster's girl-friend—as the weight of evidence seems to indicate he did—it was an act of astonishing recklessness. It would (among many other possibilities) have left him open to blackmail. But even if every accusation made about John Kennedy turns out to be absolutely true, a difference still exists between Kennedy and Clinton.

For Kennedy's excesses occurred at a time and in a country where there was every expectation his activities would be held in confidence by the press. Whatever the virtues of the then-standing "zone of privacy," President Kennedy had every reason to rely on it. With President Clinton things are very different. Ever since the "bimbo eruptions" of 1992, he has had no reason to believe that his actions would remain private. Whatever you may think of the level of scrutiny imposed by the press of the 1990s, it is a fact of life. The president's recklessness in the face of it, his lack of circumspection, is what finally distances him even from John Kennedy.

Bill Clinton's sexual indiscipline is alarming in its compulsiveness, self-indulgence, and carelessness. His relationship with Monica Lewinsky may hardly even qualify as an affair; it may be more akin to an exploitation for sexual service between the most powerful man in the world and one of a hundred young interns serving in his White House. During his 1992 appearance on *60 Minutes* when candidate Clinton admitted to having caused "pain in my marriage," he made an implicit agreement with the American people.

In the words of Clinton's former senior adviser George Stephanopoulos, "The point of the *60 Minutes* declaration was that . . . Clinton was offering a clear definition of character that the country could judge him by: 'I may not be perfect,' he was saying, 'but I'll fight for you. I'll be a president who puts people first, and I'll get up every day determined to be a better person than I was the day before.'"

Stephanopoulos goes on to say this: "If true, the allegations about the president's relationship with Monica Lewinsky show that he failed to meet the standard of character he set for himself, and shattered the promise he made to the public and the people around him."

IV

James Madison famously wrote that men are not angels, and this insight must provide context for this discussion: saintly perfection is not a prerequisite for political leadership. Human nature is fallen.

And individuals ought to be judged on the totality of their acts. In most instances, normal human frailties and personal failures should remain genuinely private matters. Nor should they necessarily cost a person his political career. For example, it is by no means clear that a political leader who on occasion drinks too much should be disqualified from holding political office. It depends on how frequently, and at what times of the day or night, the drinking occurs; whether it interferes with his ability to carry out the public business; whether it is a sign of compulsive behavior and a loss of control; and what reactions it might trigger (violent outbursts, for example). If once in a while there are a few too many drinks late in the evening, as a way to relax and unwind, that is another matter entirely.

Divorce, to take another example, may or may not be relevant, depending on what else is involved and what things it reveals. Were there acts of violence? Was the divorce bitter, cruel, and connected to abusive behavior? Or was it the case of two people gradually leading separate lives, and then finally going their separate ways? On the matter of sexual infidelity, too, finally there comes a question of balance.

Self-government depends on the capacity of free citizens to exercise reasonable judgments. To be able to look at a set of circumstances and say: it is relevant when it is relevant.

So here's a thought experiment: a president has a lurid sexual relationship with a young White House intern. The intern decides, after considerable soul-searching, to reveal the affair because she believes the actions by the president are degrading to the office, to her, and to the president's family. She learns, too, of numerous other affairs the president is having. She is not only angered to find this out, but considers his actions a sign of alarming carelessness. She begins to talk to friends about it, and word eventually makes its way to a person who happens to be a reporter at the *Washington Post*. He in turn begins to pursue leads. The White House learns that this ambitious reporter is finding out too much.

The president—the thought experiment continues—decides the story needs to be suppressed in order to maintain his political viability. He is furious that a sexual affair between two consenting adults could do irreparable harm to his presidency. He has grand policy ambitions to pursue in education, health care, tax policy, and foreign relations. He therefore, reluctantly, orders his aides to use "dirty tricks." The White House quickly swings into action.

- The president's men break into the office of a psychiatrist who has been counseling the young intern, hoping to destroy her credibility if she ever goes public with the charges. They also hire a private investigator to look into the intern's past.
- They dig up dirt on the reporter's fiancée and decide to use wiretaps on the reporter's home and work phones. White House aides even decide to pressure the IRS to begin looking into the reporter's history.
- They find out that the reporter has started to talk with a person who can corroborate key portions of the intern's story. In order to keep him quiet, the president orders "hush money" payments. The money is paid out of an account known inside the White House as "SF" (for "Slush Fund").

But slowly, inevitably, portions of the story leak out. Allegations surface. After several months, congressional hearings are called. The public begins to ask questions. And the president begins to see his support erode, overwhelmed by wave after wave of criminal allegations.

In the hope of stanching the political hemorrhage, the president agrees to hire a special prosecutor, confident that he can control the direction of the investigation. But when it turns out he can't, the president fires the special prosecutor, as well as others in his administration whom he deems to be disloyal (let's call it a "Saturday Night Massacre"). And in an attempt to keep incriminating conversations with White House aides from coming to light, the president invokes "executive privilege." But the Supreme Court rules unanimously that executive privilege does not apply when its purpose is to shield conversations between the president and his aides that may bear on a criminal investigation. It also turns out that incriminating portions of a tape recording have been erased (let's refer to it as an eighteen-and-a-half minute gap).

In other words, assume all the crimes of Watergate occurred— no, assume only *half* the crimes of Watergate occurred—but instead of the triggering event being a "third-rate burglary," assume it was a third-rate sexual relationship between a president and a young woman in the White House. Now ask yourself: in that situation, would it be right to give the president a pass? At what point do the Clinton defenders decide that crimes done in order to cover up an affair between two consenting adults are serious? Is the logic that, if sex is at the bottom, *anything* piled on top is irrelevant? Or do we decide a president—in a desperate attempt to hide acts of sexual infidelity—can commit perjury and suborn perjury, but we will draw the line at . . . what? Obstruction of justice? Wiretapping? Payments in exchange for (or threats to ensure) silence? Improper use of the IRS and CIA? And on what compelling grounds are the lines drawn, the distinctions made?

Let's therefore concede the obvious: the private lives of public figures can often be relevant. Indeed, in the case of President Clinton, as University of Virginia Professor James Ceaser has written, the distinction between the public and private realms has altogether collapsed, as "the power and prerogatives of public office [have been] employed to satisfy the public official's private desires."

Our current president seems, by a large quantity of evidence, to be possessed of several improper proclivities, sexual and moral in a large sense, and one begins to suspect that each episode is not an isolated failing but rather a symptom of something more fundamental, and quite relevant. Chronic indiscipline, compulsion, exploitation, the easy betrayal of vows, all suggest something wrong at a deep level—something habitual and beyond control. The behavior appears to be incorrigible; it does not occasion contrition, a need for absolution or change. More than events that must be judged in and of themselves, the president's pattern of sexual behavior presents itself as a series of clues to what he is.

Yes, we are, all of us, sinners. But aren't we at least supposed to struggle to do better and to be better? Bill Clinton seems to have abjured the struggle, being satisfied merely to pursue his own unruly appetites and passions. And then to justify the pursuit. And then to try and force us all to justify it, and him as well. If ever there has been a case in which adultery matters because of what it reveals about the corruption of a man's loves and his aims, as well as of his governing character—where we see, in the words of Professor Robert King, that "betrayal is a garment without seams"—it is the presidency of William Jefferson Clinton.

Chapter 2

Character

Defense of President Clinton: *Part of our contemporary* vox populi *has it that, whatever the president's character may be, our real concern—especially for the future—is the state of the national economy. One typical voter who opposed Mr. Clinton in 1996 told the* Washington Post: *"What we should be talking about is that we are going to have the first balanced budget in more than three decades. That's going to impact our children, not this sleaze that is masquerading as news." A Republican voter in Harrisburg, Pennsylvania, told reporters, "He does the job, gives a good speech, and everybody makes money." USA* Today *explained the president's high approval ratings this way: "There is universal agreement on one point: The economy is good, and they've [the public] felt it in their lives." And because the economy is good, presidential character and private conduct don't matter—at least not much.*

This argument has been extended into areas other than the economy. According to many Clinton defenders, the real test of his presidency is how we are doing on important and complex issues like education, welfare, health care, and day care. The president himself uses this argument, as when he declared at a press conference that he would not answer questions on scandal-related matters because his job was to "keep working on the people's business." Minority Leader Richard Gephardt has complained about "the time that this [Starr investigation] has taken," since it draws the attention of the country "away from the things that we most should be working on—education, health care, pensions, jobs, wages, the economy, moving the country in the right direction."

One major implication of arguments like these is that we should view the presidency through a strictly utilitarian lens. Another is that we should respect a vast zone of presidential privacy, because a president's personal life does not bear on his public duties. Indeed, the president's poll ratings are taken as evidence that this sort of "compartmentalization" is already going on. The Washington Post *summarized its findings this way: "Taken as a whole, the poll suggests an ability of the American public to compartmentalize when it comes to Clinton."*

In other words, even if Bill Clinton did all that he is accused of doing, it is essentially irrelevant to his primary job, which is to see to the well-being of the nation. Thus the conclusion earlier this year by Housing and Urban Development Secretary Andrew Cuomo: "Let's remember what's important here. The lives of the American people are more important than the personal life of the president."

Wendy Kaminer, a fellow at Radcliffe College, has gone even further, writing an article in the Boston Globe *ridiculing the idea that the president ought to be held to high moral standards. According to Ms. Kaminer, "there is something childlike and potentially dangerous about expecting the president to serve as our moral exemplar; that's what monarchs and demagogues do."*

Finally, there has even been an attempt to turn this whole issue on its head, and to redefine our understanding of morality and of moral authority altogether. During an appearance on Meet the Press, *former Clinton chief of staff Leon Panetta said: "I think the public understands what moral authority is all about. Moral authority is when a president deals with the issues that affect their families, when he deals with educating their children, when he deals with jobs, when he deals with the economy." That is to say, so-called infelicities in office are not a moral indicator of anything at all; the only such indicator is the general condition of the country, and by that criterion the president is morality incarnate.*

Response

The logic of this particular defense goes something like this: the way to judge America is above all by its economic condition; if the American people are prosperous, the president must be doing a good job; President Clinton is doing a good job on economics and many other matters, despite the various scandals attached to his name; since the scandals attending this administration are measurable only against its accomplishments, and since its accomplishments are so great, the effects of the scandals will not be long-lasting. No trail of bad consequences will survive Bill Clinton.

All are false.

I

We can all agree that economic well-being—growth, wages, inflation, the unemployment rate, and the Dow Jones Industrial

Average—is an important, legitimate issue. It was the economic "misery index," after all, that fueled Ronald Reagan's forty-four-state landslide in 1980, and the turnaround in that condition which led to his forty-nine-state landslide in 1984. Certainly the founding fathers understood the benefits of a commercial republic and argued its virtues (even as they worried that luxury and affluence might dull our moral sensibilities).

At the same time, the "people's business" is not as narrowly defined as the president and his supporters intend. No great civilization—*none*—has ever been judged great because of wealth alone. And more than any other, the American republic has stood in support of, and been governed by, a clear proposition: there are things that matter more than gold.

The United States, after all, was founded on "self-evident" truths and on an appeal to the "Laws of Nature and of Nature's God." Almost all our greatest achievements have resulted from battles waged and won over moral issues and involving our understanding of right and wrong. Although the Revolutionary War was fought in part over restrictive British policies toward the American colonies, the deep meaning of the Revolution, as the founders themselves wrote, had to do with principles and opinions, sentiments, affections, and, especially, ideals. So powerful were these ideals then and so powerful do they remain today that the words of the Declaration of Independence define much of the world's moral currency.

America's debate over slavery, the most wrenching in our history, lit the fuse that set off a great civil war. Abraham Lincoln was unwilling to accept "a house divided against itself," a nation half-slave and half-free—despite the short-term economic advantages (of which there were many) that might accrue from abiding by the status quo. And the war came. Similarly, America's civil rights struggle in the twentieth century was a campaign for justice, the redemption of a "promissory note" signed by the architects of our republic who promised that all would be guaranteed the unalienable rights of life, liberty, and the pursuit of happiness. To be sure, it was not a debate over economic efficiency.

In event after event, through the American centuries, we see moral purpose defining our highest goals and our highest achievements. Polls tell us, moreover, that Americans agree overwhelmingly about the importance of moral matters. These days, they care especially about the problem of moral decline: drug use, collapsing families, crime, callousness, vulgarity, incivility. Pollster Daniel Yankelovich reported in 1996 that "public distress about the state of our social morality has reached nearly universal proportions: 87 percent of the public fear that something is fundamentally wrong with America's moral condition." As the novelist John Updike put it, "The fact that . . . we still live well cannot ease the pain of feeling that we no longer live nobly."

Updike is right; if we have full employment and greater economic growth—if we have cities of gold and alabaster—but our children have not learned to walk in goodness, justice, and mercy, then the American experiment, no matter how gilded, will have failed. A strong economy is a good thing. But it is far from everything. That, at least, is the traditional American understanding of things.

II

Even if one is not moved by this traditional American understanding, however, there are solid arguments to be made on behalf of pursuing moral goods. Perhaps surprisingly, some of those arguments are even economic.

National prosperity, as it happens, is largely dependent upon lots of good private character. If lying, manipulation, sloth, lack of discipline, and personal irresponsibility become commonplace, the national economy grinds down. A society that produces street predators and white-collar criminals has to pay for prison cells. A society in which drug use is rampant must pay for drug treatment centers. The crack-up of families means many more foster homes and lower high school graduation rates. A society that is parsimonious in its personal charity (in terms of both time and money) will require more government welfare. Just as there are enormous financial benefits to moral health, there are enormous financial costs to moral collapse.

I am not saying anything here that most people do not already know to be true in their bones. What makes our society tick, aside from good governance and competence, is good character. And good character is not some abstraction. It is one of those tangible, very real human attributes that we know, and appreciate, when we see it.

Do Americans still acknowledge, implicitly or explicitly, that core ethical values like honesty, respect, distinguishing right and wrong—*good character*—are important and often even decisive? Of course they do. A good mother would never accept from her son the explanation that, because he did well on the Scholastic Aptitude Test, his drug habit or binge drinking doesn't matter. A good father would not dismiss casually a report card from a teacher saying that his son was excellent at math and reading but was a classroom troublemaker: rude, disruptive, stealing things, always getting into fights.

Nor are Americans in general blind to the dictates of good character in other realms. Religious congregations dismiss pastors for unethical or inappropriate private behavior, regardless of the quality of their sermons; in law enforcement, a good police commissioner will rid his department of a bigoted cop, regardless of how sterling the officer's arrest record; in the world of the military, the code of military justice demands rigid standards of personal conduct, no matter how great a soldier's prowess on the battlefield.

A colleague of mine offers the following illustration: your child goes to a high school where the SAT scores are 16 percent higher than the national average; the senior class college acceptance rate for the first and second choice of colleges is 94 percent; the girls' hockey team went to the state finals; the band was invited to the Rose Bowl Parade; and the football team is undefeated for two seasons. Under these circumstances, do you think it is acceptable for the principal to fondle young substitute teachers?

The founders—who were not utopians but eminently practical men—thought that character mattered in the presidency. A lot. Arguing for a strong executive in *Federalist No. 70*, Alexander Hamilton pointed out that while a king might avoid supervision by hiding behind a privy council, the American president assumes an extraordinary degree of responsibility. "From the very circumstances of his being alone," Hamilton wrote, the president "will be more narrowly watched and more readily suspected." The standard in the executive branch was supposed to be different, *higher*, than for the legislative and judicial branches.

The founders (like the ancient Greeks) believed it was important that the head of the good polity be a man of good character, and they advocated that the office of the presidency be filled by persons whose "reputation for integrity inspires and merits confidence." The intimate connection between private and public character was understood as a form of integrity, whose root word is *integer*, meaning "whole." The leader must be whole; he cannot have his public character be honest and his private character be deceitful. "The purity of his private character gave effulgence to his public virtues," were the beautiful words said of George Washington upon his death.

Here an important clarification needs to be made: in a president good character is not everything. There are other traits to which the public should look as well: a solid record of achievement; a grounded and coherent political philosophy; a strong command of issues; an analytical mind; the ability to recruit and keep talented advisers; powerful rhetorical abilities; the capacity to mobilize public opinion and shape sentiments; and the ability to anticipate world events. People of good character can be bad presidents, and people of average character can be fine presidents.

We would not want and should not create a political culture in which personal failure or every character flaw automatically disqualified a person seeking high public office. And public officials (like everyone else) also deserve a legitimate zone of personal privacy. Christian doctrine teaches that all have sinned and fall short. Everybody has flaws, and many of us have serious flaws.

What we need is a realistic, disinterested view of whether such flaws are, or might be, relevant to the highest public office. Sometimes they are. A president whose character manifests itself in patterns of reckless personal conduct, deceit, abuse of power, and contempt for the rule of law cannot be a good president. These aspects of character, in this combination, are surely relevant. Here is John Adams: "Rulers are no more than attorneys, agents, and trustees, for the people; and if the cause, the interest and trust, is insidiously betrayed, or wantonly trifled away, the people have a right to revoke the authority that they themselves have deputed."

III

The idea that the president should be a man of good character remained strong for many years in the early republic. But by the end of the nineteenth century and through the twentieth, our concept of political leadership began to shift. Management skills began to take priority over character; the idea was that a new and more "progressive" science of government would make reliance on good men unnecessary. This disjunction continued to take root through the following decades, to the point where many people today treat private and public character as entirely separate and unrelated categories.

Enter compartmentalization. To recall the words of the *Washington Post* poll from earlier this year, the American people are remarkably able "to compartmentalize when it comes to Clinton." So the president receives very high job approval ratings (60-plus percent) even as he receives extremely low ratings on the question of whether he has high personal moral and ethical standards (24 percent).

What are we to make of presidential compartmentalization—or what we might better call "presidential character exemption"? Let us take it compartment by compartment.

In the area of policy management—that is, job performance—President Clinton's supporters consider him to be a man almost without parallel, and as evidence they cite the impressive progress we have made under his stewardship. Since, for the sake of argument, I am going to grant them their premise, I should first register my belief that it happens to be, in several areas at least, a false one. I have strong, fundamental criticisms of his policies.

In a number of crucial areas, I believe, the president has demonstrably harmed the national interest: cutting defense spending to a dangerously low level; adamantly refusing to move ahead with a strategic missile defense; pursuing a flaccid and often wrongheaded foreign policy, particularly in the area of human rights and with respect to countries like Iraq, China, Sudan, Russia, Pakistan, India, and Somalia; emasculating the federal anti-drug effort; supporting racial quotas and set-asides; siding time after time with the education unions to block commonsense education reforms; and refusing to ban even partial-birth abortions.

But to repeat: for the sake of argument, assume I am wrong about this and President Clinton does deserve much credit for what is right with the country. Then what? Even if you think he is the greatest policy president ever, it does not change what is at stake in this particular context. In early 1974, as the Watergate scandal was beginning to engulf his presidency, Richard Nixon invoked an almost identical argument to the one used by Clinton defenders. People, he said, could "wallow in Watergate" if they chose to, but there were important affairs of state to which he had to attend. Should we have ignored President Nixon's misconduct because of his historic opening to communist China, or because of the danger of war in the Middle East, or because he may have been a skillful practitioner of foreign policy in general?

The values-free standard "effectiveness in office" cannot—it must not—trump everything else. In a constitutional government, there must be some important norms to which we adhere and to which we hold our leaders, whether things are going splendidly or not. We did not give up on them during the Nixon era, and we cannot give up on them in the Clinton era. The most important thing is not policies on day care or other matters; it is maintaining fidelity to the Constitution and that old, great, American idea that no one, not even a king, is above the law.

IV

"Moral authority is when a president deals with the issues that affect [people's] families, when he deals with educating their children, when he deals with jobs, when he deals with the economy." Thus Leon Panetta. But there is much more to moral authority than that. We—all of us, but especially the young—need around us individuals who possess a certain nobility, a largeness of soul, and qualities of human excellence worth imitating and striving for. Every parent knows this, which is why parents are concerned with both the company their children keep, and the role models they choose. Children watch what we do as well as what we say, and if we expect them to take morality seriously, they must see adults taking it seriously.

The extraordinary political appeal of General Colin Powell is rooted in his rock-solid character, his wartime valor, his faithfulness as a husband and father. He is the type of man that mothers can point to and say to their children, "Here is a man who fought for his country, honors his wife, loves his family. Be like that man." Thus it was said of General Washington: "His example was as edifying to all around him as were the effects of that example lasting."

Character education depends not only on the articulation of ideals and convictions, but on the behavior of those in authority. This is why the president is a role model, whether he likes it or not, and why Wendy Kaminer is dead wrong when she writes that there is something "childlike and potentially dangerous" in expecting a president to have high moral standards. That is obviously not his only responsibility. Nor is it his first responsibility. But it *is* a responsibility he cannot shirk.

The basketball star Charles Barkley insists that sports figures ought not be role models for children. I believe Barkley is wrong— but even if he is right, the one public figure who cannot dodge his responsibility as a role model is the president. It is worth noting that the president—whoever he is—is almost always voted the most admired man in America, not just because he is so well-known, but because of the prestige of the office itself. What he does, and who he is, matter.

It is true that the bond of trust between a president and the American people matters most when times require some measure of sacrifice or hardship; it is then that we most need someone who is reliable, dependable, believable. But the implicit argument that a president can compromise his moral authority in a time of peace and prosperity is more than a misunderstanding; it is absurd. Moral authority once having been compromised, who can with confidence expect it to be magically available in a time when sacrifice is needed?

Besides, there are countless instances even in placid times like ours when citizens are asked to accept what the president says, when he must tap into a reservoir of trust and goodwill, of faith in his word. On the issue of the recent sale of high technology to China, the charge is that venality compromised national security. President Clinton denied those accusations. But we know that we cannot trust his denial, because, as I will illustrate in greater detail in the next section of this chapter, we cannot trust his word.

The president tells us that "we are encouraged about [Iraq's] level of compliance so far with the U.N. inspections." But through experience we know that we cannot trust this statement, because we cannot trust his word. And so on.

In general, if the president's word cannot be trusted—an issue of character—voters cannot take seriously his election platform or his campaign promises—an issue of public duty. Words are deconstructed, promises emptied of meaning. Politics is reduced to a mere game. It is all very straightforward: if a man's word means nothing, it means nothing. It is folly to believe otherwise.

President Clinton knows this as well as anyone. He himself has decried a "changing culture that desensitizes our children to violence." True enough. A culture can desensitize children, and adults, too, to lots of things—not just violence, but dishonesty and lack of accountability among those who hold high public office. What we need in our president is one who stands *against* destructive cultural norms, not one who embodies, manipulates, and exploits them.

Earlier this year, an elementary school counselor told *USA Today* that publicity about the president's alleged behavior sent a damaging message to the children she counsels. "If we had a group of 8, 9, 10, 11-year olds sitting around this table, 99% of them would say, 'No big deal, everybody does it.' This is what has happened." In a *Time* magazine cover story, sixth-, seventh-, and eighth-grade boys at a Denver middle school rationalize a sharp rise in lewd language, groping, pinching, and bra-snapping this way: "If the president can do it, why can't we?"

Bill Clinton's behavior has started seeping into the culture. In Columbus, Ohio, ads for a car dealer named Bobby's use a Monica Lewinsky look-alike (complete with "Secret Service" agents) saying, "Hi, I'm the new intern . . . If you want to get serviced late at night during the week, Bobby's open all the way until midnight." David Letterman's and Jay Leno's monologues, which closely track current political happenings, are much raunchier and sexually explicit than ever before. On NBC's *Today* show, Katie Couric and Matt Lauer warned viewers earlier this year that part of a discussion about President Clinton's relationship with Monica Lewinsky might be graphic, and parents might "want to turn down the volume" on their TV sets. According to Jeff Zucker, the show's producer, "I don't remember the last time we had to issue a warning about sex. . . . Children are watching the show with their parents, eating breakfast before they go to school."

During the 1998 Academy Awards, host Billy Crystal summed things up this way: "So much has changed in a year. A year ago the White House was complaining there was too much sex in *Hollywood*." It is a sad state of affairs indeed when Hollywood is able to make a joke from a position of moral superiority. But that is where we are.

V

I have been saying that public efficacy is an important but incomplete measuring stick, that the president of the United States must be evaluated by other measures as well. But as it turns out, this president's private conduct has had, and continues to have, a profound impact on his much-touted talent for public governance. In fact, there is a seamless web of deceit that connects Bill Clinton's private and public life, his private failings and his

public failings. He is among the *least* compartmentalized presidents ever. His "private" character is not only relevant to his mode
of governance; it is inseparable from it.

In retrospect, we received plenty of warning signs of Bill Clinton's problems with veracity. Consider, for the moment, his handling of a key issue during the 1992 presidential campaign: his
relation as a young man to the Vietnam War and the military draft.
Set aside the merits of the war itself. What we see is how, in the
world of Bill Clinton (as it had been years before in the world of
Richard Nixon), lies beget lies.

To recapitulate: in a December 1991 interview with the *Washington Post,* then-Governor Clinton said, "I've always been interested
in and supportive of the military. That is something, you know, in
some ways I wish I'd been a part of it. I wound up just going through
the lottery and it was just a pure fluke that I wasn't called."

A few months later, Mr. Clinton was asked whether he had not,
in fact, received an induction letter from the army. He told the *Los
Angeles Times,* "It was simply a fluke I wasn't called and there are
no facts to the contrary."

But there *were* facts to the contrary. Hard evidence surfaced
that Bill Clinton had received an induction letter from the army.
When asked why he did not previously reveal the fact, Mr. Clinton
said, "It just never occurred to me to make anything of it one way
or the other, since it was just a routine matter."

There is more. In September 1992 candidate Clinton told
reporters he had "never received any unusual or favorable treatment" in his effort to avoid serving in Vietnam. But later that
month his campaign organization was forced to acknowledge
(because of newly discovered archive documents) that in 1969
Clinton had indeed asked for help from Arkansas Senator J.
William Fulbright's office. It was on the basis of his avowed intent
to join the University of Arkansas ROTC that he was in fact
granted a draft deferment; but then he backed out of his commit-

ment and instead enrolled at Yale Law School, leading Lieutenant Colonel Eugene Holmes, the ROTC commander at Arkansas, to charge that Bill Clinton had lied to him about his intentions.

Similarly, the *Los Angeles Times* reported in September 1992 that Mr. Clinton's uncle had helped him win a reserve unit position. "It's all news to me," Mr. Clinton responded, before then being forced to again reverse himself, saying he had learned only six months earlier of his uncle's lobbying to help him avoid military service. And then came a classic Clinton maneuver, of the I-didn't-do-it-and-even-if-I-did-it-doesn't-matter variety:

"It's amazing to me that even if all this stuff was true, it doesn't change anything about what I did or knew at the time. . . . You've got a feeding frenzy on about something that even if it's true, it doesn't amount to a hill of beans. I knew nothing about it and it does not affect the truth that I have told about the facts of the draft situation. None of the facts of my story have changed."

In the early 1970s, Clinton was so concerned about the possible repercussions of a December 1969 letter he had written to Colonel Holmes (thanking the ROTC colonel for "saving" him from the draft) that he arranged to have the original destroyed. But he did not know that a copy had been made. According to David Maraniss, the respected Clinton biographer, an ROTC drill instructor had warned Clinton that reporters were asking about such a letter, and Clinton replied: "Don't worry about that, I've put that one to bed."

In that 1969 letter to Colonel Holmes, Clinton, who would later state unequivocally that he was never opposed to the draft, wrote, "From my work I came to believe that the draft system itself is illegitimate. . . ." In a 1994 interview with NBC's Tom Brokaw, President Clinton brazenly declared that "all the people who grew up in my generation were hurt maybe worse than any other generation could have been by their ambivalence over Vietnam, because we all love the military so much." A younger and presumably not yet ambivalent Clinton had written to Colonel Holmes about "loathing the military."

On and on it goes, in matters ranging from sexual affairs (Gennifer Flowers) to marijuana ("I didn't inhale") to you name it. But the point is clear enough, and it is intimately tied to the Clinton style of governance. In a moment of admirable candor, Democratic Senator Bob Kerrey said, "Clinton's an unusually good liar. Unusually good." And in 1992, the Reverend Jesse Jackson put it this way: "I can maybe work with him, but I know now who he is, what he is. There's *nothin'* he won't do. He's immune to shame. Move past all the nice posturing and get really down in there in him, you find absolutely nothing . . . nothing but an appetite."

This pattern of mendacity—of *public* shamelessness—has not gone unnoticed by the press. Ruth Marcus of the *Washington Post* wrote in 1994, "To borrow a phrase from the law of libel, the Clinton White House often seems to be following a pattern of knowing or reckless disregard for the truth. . . . Nineteen months of repeated falsehoods and half-truths have corroded the relationship between this White House and the reporters who cover it."

Bob Woodward of Watergate fame put it this way: "People feel, and I think rightly, that they're not being leveled with. . . . There is this tendency in Clinton which you see all through his life of, 'How do we spin our way out of it? How do we put out 10 percent of the truth? How do we try to conceal or delay or obfuscate?' And that is a profound problem."

Michael Kelly, then of the *New York Times*, wrote, "Mr. Clinton's tendency to make misleading statements, renege on promises, and waffle on difficult questions has been a part of the story of his record in matters of public policy and politics, *not just in personal terms*" (emphasis added).

And in 1994 Joe Klein, then a columnist for *Newsweek* magazine, wrote a cover story, "The Politics of Promiscuity," that contained a devastating indictment of Bill Clinton: "They haven't gotten him yet. They may never. But a clear pattern has emerged—of delay, of obfuscation, of lawyering the truth. The litany of offenses is as familiar as it is depressing. . . . With the Clintons, the story *always* is subject to further revision. The misstatements are always incremental. The 'misunderstandings' are always innocent— casual, irregular: promiscuous. Trust is squandered in dribs and drabs. Does this sort of behavior also infect the president's public life, his formulation of policy? Clearly, it does."

Clearly, it still does, and in numerous ways, both obvious and subtle. To judge by recent examples, the president's ability to govern, in which his defenders take such pride, has been manifestly compromised by his indifference to truth. Earlier this year the president's foreign policy team went to Ohio State to host a "town hall meeting," the purpose of which was to demonstrate that the American people were solidly behind the administration's policy toward Iraq's Saddam Hussein; the program was intentionally aired on CNN, to ensure a worldwide audience. But several people in the audience disrupted the proceedings, and others grilled Secretary of State Madeleine Albright, Secretary of Defense William Cohen, and National Security Adviser Samuel Berger, who, to put it charitably, lost control of the event. It turned out to be a public relations debacle.

Now, there are very few if any people in public life today as adept as the president in leading such a town hall meeting, and the Ohio State event was exactly the kind of forum at which he excels. But the president wasn't there; he was obviously kept away because the White House feared he would be asked questions about the Monica Lewinsky story. This most prolix of presidents was unable to articulate and defend his own national security aims, unable to mobilize public sentiment on behalf of his policy, unable to show up at a public forum.

For those who might still argue that private behavior does not affect public duties, consider that in the Supreme Court case *Clinton v. Jones,* Mr. Clinton's lawyers argued for a delay until his term ended precisely because a hearing of the case would interfere with the president's performance of his constitutional duties. On another matter, White House counsel Charles F. C. Ruff told the U.S. District Court that Kenneth Starr's investigation of the Lewinsky case was "inextricably intertwined with the daily presidential agenda, and thus has a substantial impact on the president's ability to discharge his obligations." And in a friend-of-the-court brief, Attorney General Janet Reno wrote that the independent counsel's "investigation of 'private' conduct—the Monica Lewinsky and Jones litigation matters—has had a substantial impact on the president's performance of official duties."

The upshot is that in Bill Clinton we have a president who cannot seem to stop himself from tunneling underneath the supposed wall dividing private and public behavior. And so we should not be surprised that the wall often collapses. A very great deal of public wrongdoing has arisen from attempts to advance private personal gain and appetites, whether sexual, financial, or political. It is easy to see why the president's defenders have worked so hard to try to separate—to compartmentalize—his public and private behaviors. Once "decompartmentalized," the list of Clinton scandals is very large indeed:

- The Clinton administration, in order to replace the White House Travel Office with its own people, improperly used the FBI to bolster false claims of financial malfeasance and attempted to involve the IRS in firing travel office personnel.
- President Clinton's top advisers and confidants mounted a campaign to help find lucrative employment (totaling well over a half-million dollars) for Associate Attorney General

Webster Hubbell after he resigned in disgrace—and before
Hubbell began withholding important personal financial
documents from Whitewater investigators.

- Three Arkansas state troopers have testified under oath that
  they or their families were threatened by Clinton associates
  with dire consequences if they revealed the fact that they
  had procured women for then-Governor Clinton.

- Dolly Kyle Browning has said under penalty of perjury that
  her own brother, a 1992 Clinton campaign worker, warned
  her that if she talked about her alleged sexual relationship
  with Bill Clinton, "we will destroy you."

- Reelection avarice appears to have compromised national
  security by permitting the transfer of sensitive satellite technology to China; allowed a man described by the president's
  own National Security Council as a "hustler" to make more
  than fifty visits to the White House; enabled Roger Tamraz,
  an international fugitive and a major donor to the Democratic
  party, to be invited to the White House on numerous occasions over the objections of the NSC; led to the president's
  raising illegal "soft money"; and led to the misuse of a White
  House database.

- Highly improper, and highly suspicious, acquisition of more
  than nine hundred raw FBI files on political opponents came
  to light (two Secret Service agents contradicted White House
  claims that the files were obtained inadvertently by a staffer
  who unknowingly used an outdated list of White House
  employees supplied by the Secret Service).

At trial, members of the criminal bar always attempt to exclude
evidence of other crimes of which the defendant may have been
accused. So, too, in the public debate now going on, do the public
defenders of the president of the United States. They should not be

allowed to do so. These matters are of a piece, part of an unmistakable pattern with which we are all too familiar.

VI

Let's turn to the final component of the arguments offered by those determined not to be outraged by the president. These apologists may concede that the proper measure of the president is more than the prosperity of the nation, that character matters (somewhat). They may even concede that Bill Clinton's capacity for governance has been impeded (somewhat) by his propensity for private deceit. Still, they say, whatever damage may have been done will be limited to this administration itself. There will be no lasting effects.

This, too, is false.

During moments of crisis, of unfolding scandal, people watch closely. They learn from what they see. And they often embrace a prevailing attitude and ethos, and employ what seems to work for others. So it matters if the legacy of the president is that the ends justify the means; that rules do not apply across the board; that lawlessness can be excused. It matters, too, if we demean the presidency by lowering our standards of expectations for the office and by redefining moral authority down. It matters if truth becomes incidental, and public office is used to cover up private misdeeds. And it matters if we treat a president as if he were a king, above the law.

John Dean said of Watergate: "If Watergate had succeeded, what would have been put into the system for years to come? People thinking the way Richard Nixon thought, and thinking that is the way it should be. It would have been a travesty; it would have been frightening."

Defenders of both Richard Nixon and of Bill Clinton forget that the cost of raising the threshold of moral outrage is paid out over generations—and with compound interest. How much of the political cynicism that today says "they all do it" can be laid at the feet of actions committed twenty-five years ago during the Watergate scandal? Twenty-five years from today, what will be the cost of the Clinton scandals to the America of our children and grandchildren?

Chapter 3

Politics

Defense of President Clinton: *The reason Bill Clinton's behavior has become an object of scrutiny, we are told, has to do entirely with partisan politics: his governing agenda is anathema to conservatives. As First Lady Hillary Clinton said on the* Today *show, the president's many scandals arise from but a single cause: "this vast right-wing conspiracy that has been conspiring against my husband since the day he announced for president."*

More broadly, Democrats bemoan the damage conservatives and Republicans are doing to our political culture. According to Minority Leader Gephardt, "I think [Republicans] are . . . transfixed with one thing and one thing only, and that's the political destruction of the president." Echoing the theme, former White House counsel Jack Quinn said, "What I think has happened over the last several years is just a remarkable attack on the institution of the presidency." And senior presidential aide Rahm Emanuel put it this way: "I think that this president has always chosen the field of ideas, not the field of insults, the fields of progress over politics. Someone wants to choose insults and politics over ideas and also progress; that's their course."

A second argument made by President Clinton's defenders sounds in some ways like the opposite of the first but comes out in essentially the same place. Acknowledging that an admirable politician can sometimes do distasteful things, the president's supporters admonish us that the point of politics is to advance a cherished and important cause. This explains why the selfsame feminists could react with fury against Justice Clarence Thomas and then support President Clinton when he became the one being charged with sexual harassment.

The archetypical expression of this sentiment comes from political commentator and feminist Susan Estrich. In an exchange with the journalist Stuart Taylor, who had marshaled an impressive array of facts to bolster the sexual harassment claims of Paula Jones, Ms. Estrich declared, "You believe in principle. I believe in politics"—meaning, I believe in using whatever political means may be necessary to achieve the ends of feminism. Or as Eleanor Smeal, president of the Feminist Majority Fund, explained, "We're trying to think of the bigger picture, think about what's best for women." To author Susan Faludi, the women who have accused the president of inappropriate sexual conduct "are not considering the advancement of their sex" and are violating a "defining trait of feminism: sisterhood."

A third defense offered on behalf of the president combines the first two in a formulation that is meant to capture a larger truth about political life: "they all do it." "I wasn't the biggest Clinton fan," a voter from Glenside, Pennsylvania, told the New York Times. "But when I see all the things that he's been able to do, it just seems that someone is going to great lengths to ruin his day. Presidents in the past have done much worse." Another voter told the Washington Post, "I'm a Republican, and I think [Clinton's] *a hypocrite the way he always comes out for family values, . . . but I don't think he's really any more guilty than anyone else."* Robert Kuttner, co-editor of the magazine The American Prospect, reported the wisdom he had gleaned from "the proverbial taxi driver": *"They all do it. What do you expect of politicians?"*

In other words, even if President Clinton is guilty of criminal as well as sexual wrongdoing, presidents and public officials are routinely expected to engage in corruption, sexual misconduct, and inappropriate behavior. This helps to account for the low esteem in which politicians are held these days by the American public.

Response

This argument is that President Clinton has not done anything wrong, and his ethical troubles are the result of fiercely partisan, and wholly inappropriate, attacks; Republicans are coarsening our political culture with these attacks; President Clinton's enlightened policies—particularly on social issues—make him deserving of support even if he did something inappropriate; and if Mr. Clinton did engage in wrongdoing, so what? They all do it anyway. I will deal with each argument in turn.

I

Is there a "vast right-wing conspiracy" that has been "conspiring" against Bill Clinton since the day he announced for president? And if so, is it responsible for manufacturing the scandals that have wounded the Clinton presidency? The short answer to both questions is: no.

In the interview she gave to the *Today* show immediately after the Lewinsky story broke, Mrs. Clinton asserted that the various

Clinton-related scandals were the result of more than simply a "politically motivated prosecutor who is allied with the right-wing opponents of my husband." She warned of the conspiracy's ominous size. "We're talking about—but it's the whole operation," Mrs. Clinton said. "It's—it's not just one person, it's an entire operation."

The next day, on *Good Morning America*, Mrs. Clinton amplified her position. "I don't think there's any doubt that there are professional forces on the right at work for their own purposes and profit. There are just so many curious relationships among a lot of people, and various institutes and entities. And I think that that deserves thorough investigation." And more: "One of my husband's favorite old Southern sayings [is] . . . if you find a turtle on a fence post, it didn't get there by accident. And I just look at the landscape around here, and I see just lots of big old turtles sitting on lots of fence posts. . . . there's just a lot going on behind the scenes and kind of under the radar screen that I think the American public has a right to know."

Mrs. Clinton's charges are either intentionally preposterous or unintentionally paranoid. Either way, they themselves serve a narrow and partisan political purpose. They are designed to change the subject, to divert attention from her husband's very real scandal-related problems to the alleged politics of those who are focusing on them. But consider the argument. Was a "vast right-wing conspiracy" responsible for the *Washington Post*'s and *Newsweek*'s breaking of the Lewinsky story? Was it responsible for making Kathleen Willey, a Democrat and a supporter of Mr. Clinton, come forward to testify that she had been sexually accosted by the president? Was it responsible for adding the phrase "bimbo eruptions" to our political lexicon? Was it, for that matter, responsible for the 1992 *New York Times* story that introduced the nation to the Whitewater scandal?

The "vast right-wing conspiracy" posited by Mrs. Clinton must be vast indeed. Its members would seem to include Monica Lewinsky,

Kathleen Willey, Gennifer Flowers, former California Governor Jerry Brown, Susan McDougal, Johnny Chung, several unnamed Chinese government officials, former White House security chief Craig Livingstone, White House counsel Bernard Nussbaum, Judge Norma Holloway Johnson, reporters and editorial writers from the *New York Times*, the *Washington Post*, and *Newsweek* magazine, the television networks, and so on and so forth. To sustain Mrs. Clinton's claim, the conspiracy responsible for the scandals swirling around her husband would have to be of such a diverse and comprehensive nature— involving media outlets, the world of law enforcement, the courts, women who have worked with or for the president, foreign nationals, and even foreign countries—as to constitute not a right-wing conspiracy but a world conspiracy, bordering on the intergalactic.

It is clearly true, and publicly known, that many conservatives *are* united in their disagreement with President Clinton, a disagreement that for a much smaller number borders on contempt. But is conservative animus toward President Clinton greater than liberal animus toward Presidents Nixon and Reagan in their time? Surely not. It is a political fact that presidents of one party tend to energize the base of another in opposition; that is predictable, since the base of each party tends to have the most deeply held convictions.

In any event, conservative "anti-Clinton" sentiments run across a wide spectrum. A few anti-Clinton conservatives are nutty. There are probably even anti-Clinton nuts who conspire together. But the nutty ones not only do not define the conservative movement, they do not even comprise much of it. The overwhelming majority of the president's conservative critics—commentators, columnists, writers, newspaper editorialists, think tank scholars, politicians—are responsible men and women. The others, the nuts, are on the fringe, in the dark, exerting almost no influence except by hurting the cause they profess to believe in.

Mrs. Clinton is resorting to an old trick: attempting to discredit an argument by tethering it to its most extreme proponents.

A conservative version of this would be to assert that the critics of President Reagan's defense buildup were tools of the communists. Did some Reagan critics have Soviet sympathies? Yes. Did most? Of course not. Should responsible anti-Reagan arguments have been discredited because some extremists embraced them for their own purposes? No.

One obvious riposte to Mrs. Clinton's conspiracy charge is that Richard Nixon had enemies, too. They included anti–Vietnam War protesters, academics, people in the literary world, some in the media, and some Democrats. Before Mr. Nixon's resignation, Republican Senator Carl Curtis of Nebraska, a staunch Nixon defender, blamed Watergate on the "get-Nixon crowd, including those who continue to conduct a trial by press." And there *was* a "get-Nixon crowd"; the problem for Nixon was that it didn't break into Democratic party headquarters at the Watergate. His people did.

Nixon's secretary of state, Henry Kissinger, once quoted wryly a crack by the poet Delmore Schwartz: even paranoids have real enemies. President Nixon assuredly had real enemies. And President Clinton has real enemies, too, even a few irresponsible ones. But for a powerful public figure like the first lady to smear all her husband's critics with the charge of participating in a conspiracy is itself irresponsible—in a democracy, arguably it is the height of irresponsibility. Broad freedom of speech, after all, entails certain responsibilities; public figures above all must take care not to make false and malicious claims that set citizen against citizen. That is the result, intended or not, of Mrs. Clinton's fantastic claim.

II

Clinton loyalists assert that Republicans in general, and Kenneth Starr in particular, are damaging our political culture. Mr. Starr, in the words of presidential confidant Paul Begala, is "snooping into people's private lives. And that is abhorrent, and

that is wrong." Senior Clinton adviser Rahm Emanuel has casti-
gated Mr. Starr for having "bullied and intimidated" people.
Senior White House aide Sidney Blumenthal accuses Starr of
using "the instruments of intimidation and smear without
restraint."

I will deal in detail with Judge Starr in the next chapter. But the
first thing to recognize here is that the shoe is very much on
the other foot. Few presidents in the modern era have "bullied and
intimidated" as frequently and promiscuously as has Mr. Clinton
and those acting on his behalf. Mr. Begala's stated views
notwithstanding, they appear to be old hands at reputation-
destroying tactics.

In Arkansas, we learn, state troopers who served on then–
Governor Clinton's security detail have sworn under oath that they
procured women for him. As I mentioned in the previous chapter,
three state troopers have testified under oath that they or their families were threatened by Clinton associates if they talked, and
Dolly Kyle Browning has said under penalty of perjury that her
brother, a 1992 Clinton campaign worker, warned her that if she
talked about her alleged sexual relationship with Mr. Clinton, "we
will destroy you."

Earlier this year Dick Morris, President Clinton's longtime
political adviser and confidant, who in 1996 was embroiled in a
sex scandal of his own, appeared on CNBC's *Equal Time* and had
this to say about the 1992 presidential campaign:

"Under Betsey Wright's supervision in the 1992 Clinton campaign, there was an entire operation funded with over $100,000 of
campaign money, which included federal matching funds, to hire
private detectives to go into the personal lives of women who were
alleged to have [had] sex with Bill Clinton. To develop compromis-
ing material—blackmailing information, basically—to coerce
them into signing affidavits saying that they did not have sex with
Bill Clinton."

In Morris's words, there was "a Nixonian pattern here of using federal money to hire private investigators to investigate innocent private citizens to develop blackmail material to compromise them to get them to lie under oath." According to Morris, the operation was run by Jack Palladino, a San Francisco attorney who heads one of the nation's most successful private investigative firms. Elsewhere Morris has described "a kind of secret police going on here that goes back to the 1992 Democratic primary campaign that's simply revolting. It is absolutely chilling."

There is more. Democrat William Bradley, who has advised (among others) Gary Hart and Jerry Brown, has said that no other Democrat in his memory has made such extensive use of investigative firms as has Bill Clinton. According to Bradley, "A principal figure in this secret operation is Terry Lenzner, one of the most powerful and dreaded private investigators in the world. . . . Lenzner's work for Clinton goes back at least to 1991. During then–Governor Clinton's campaign for the 1992 Democratic presidential nomination, Lenzner investigated then–New York Governor Mario Cuomo (Clinton's most feared potential rival), former California Governor Jerry Brown (his most troublesome actual rival) and others."

Terry Lenzner's name is in the mix again today. On February 22 of this year, the administration issued a categorical denial that either the White House "or any of President Clinton's private attorneys has hired or authorized any private investigator to look into the background of . . . investigators, prosecutors or reporters." The next day, however, Lenzner said that his firm, Investigative Group Inc., had been retained by the law firm representing Mr. Clinton in the Starr investigation, adding that if his investigators were looking into the backgrounds of members of Mr. Starr's staff, "there was nothing inappropriate about that."

Maybe there is. Michael Kelly, the editor of *National Journal*, has written about White House efforts to undermine the authority of the independent counsel's office by intimidating prosecutors. During a one-month period, the office received almost one hundred calls from reporters inquiring about false and damaging accusations against its prosecutors. The calls ranged from accusations of professional misconduct to sex smears.

John Brummett, a columnist for the *Arkansas Democrat-Gazette*, writes that he was visited by a Clinton loyalist who passed along this tip: "He wondered if I'd heard anything about Starr having an affair with a Little Rock woman he named." An Arkansas attorney received similar calls (the rumors were false). *Time* magazine reporters received tips about the "workplace and sexual histories of the prosecutors." The magazine describes a "clandestine war" of "telephone calls from out-of-town lawyers who urged reporters to look at this old federal case or that sealed police report. Next came the mystery faxes, great piles of inky black clippings, detailing the dubious investigative habits of the men who work for Kenneth Starr."

Former senior Clinton aide George Stephanopoulos warned earlier this year that "White House allies are already starting to whisper about what I'll call the Ellen Rometsch strategy. . . . She was a girlfriend of John F. Kennedy, who also happened to be an East German spy. And Robert Kennedy was charged with getting her out of the country and also getting John Edgar Hoover to go to the Congress and say, 'Don't you investigate this, because if you do, we're going to open up everybody's closet.' And I think that in the long run, [the president's defenders] have a deterrent strategy."

This is very ugly stuff—particularly ugly coming from a president who bemoans the loss of civility in American politics. Who warned America about a "toxic atmosphere of cynicism" created by politicians. Who portrays himself as a national unifier and a "repairer of the breach." Who last year urged Washington to follow the scriptural injunction, "Never pay back evil for evil to anyone." And who told a National Prayer Breakfast gathering that "sometimes I think the commandment we most like to overlook in this city is, 'Thou shall not bear false witness.'" President Clinton could put an end to this ugly stuff; he could demand that his people stop the smears, the smash-mouth tactics, the declarations of "war," the tarnishing of women's reputations. But he won't, because he believes these types of tactics advance his immediate self-interest. Well, perhaps they do. And pity the fact that it harms the national interest. In the world of Bill Clinton, it seems, sometimes that is the price for maintaining political viability.

III

To Jack Quinn, the former White House counsel, the events of the last few years constitute "a remarkable attack on the institution of the presidency." In fact, I am not aware of any leading Republican who has attacked the *institution* of the presidency. What has happened is that Republicans have made very pointed criticisms of Bill Clinton, who temporarily occupies the office of the presidency. These are two very different things. I presume that Mr. Quinn does not think that imposing a moratorium on presidential criticism is a good idea in a free country. And to the extent that the institution of the presidency has been harmed, it is Mr. Clinton who is responsible. He has inflicted institutional damage by inestimably lowering the office's aura, esteem, and respect, and by allowing specious legal, constitutional, and moral arguments to be made on his behalf.

As for Rahm Emanuel, he claims that public discourse has been harmed because some people have chosen "insults" over "ideas" and "politics" over "progress." Mr. Emanuel's boss, Bill Clinton, actually urged Americans in 1995 to speak out against such "purveyors of hatred and division, the promoters of paranoia." Good idea. But what then shall he do with his own "spiritual adviser," the Reverend Jesse Jackson? Few if any prominent public figures have made greater use of sulfurous, and downright nasty language.

Among other things, Reverend Jackson has claimed that the Christian Coalition was a strong force in the slaveholding South, and later provided a "suitable, scientific, theological rationale" for the Holocaust. He equates American conservatism with South African apartheid and Nazism. He has called California Governor Pete Wilson the "Susan Smith of national politics,"* and compared him to the notorious racist sheriff of Birmingham, Bull Connor. He has likened conservative Supreme Court justices to arsonists of the Ku Klux Klan; and accused the chairman of the California Civil Rights Initiative, Ward Connerly, who happens to be black, of being a "house slave" and a "puppet of the white man."

But wait a minute, Clinton defenders say: look at the ugly stuff coming from *anti*-Clinton quarters. To which my response is: yes, there is such stuff, and it should stop. Though the tactics of Mr. Clinton's advocates are contributing mightily to the coarse state of our political culture, they are not solely responsible for it, and they are not the only ones who resort to such practices.

I am not referring merely to things like *The Clinton Chronicles*, a low-budget, poor-quality video claiming that President Clinton was responsible for murder; I publicly criticized this video at the time of its release. Or to one Republican congressman's vulgar reference to the president as a "scumbag," or to Dan Quayle's quip that the centerpiece of a Republican anti-crime proposal should be "three interns and you're out."

I am also referring to those Clinton critics who revel in what is happening to the president, and who see much humor in the president's troubles. Ad hominem criticism, done in a destructive

---

*Susan Smith is the South Carolina woman who in 1994 murdered her two children, and falsely alleged they had been kidnapped by a black man.

spirit, with the intent to slash and burn, is profoundly harmful to public life. Nor is there joy in scandal, particularly in presidential scandal, and particularly in presidential scandal that has within it so much tawdriness. *Schadenfreude* may be satisfying on a certain level, but it is unnecessarily divisive and engenders cynicism. Almost everyone in our political class has been cut by its shards.

At the same time, mine is not a counsel against criticism that is tough as well as fair. In my judgment, it is far worse to excuse wrongdoing, watch ethical standards sink, and allow justifiable outrage to die than to confront wrongdoing. It was better that President Nixon be forced to resign than that the crimes of Watergate be allowed to go unpunished. Justice even when it prevails can be tinged with poignancy and sadness, but justice needs to be done. That is what the great majority of President Clinton's conservative critics believe, and in that spirit they try to comport themselves.

IV

The next line of defense against so-called partisan attacks on the president is to answer them in kind—that is, in a wholly partisan spirit—while also claiming the high ground of principle. Thus, we are told that President Clinton deserves the unwavering support of his allies because politics, reduced to its essence, is about advancing one's cause, regardless of the means utilized. This is a variant of what philosophers call consequentialism, a moral theory that judges the rightness and wrongness of an act solely on the results the act produces. To nonphilosophers, this is known as "the ends justify the means."

For feminists, the "end" that earns (almost) unwavering support is the president's commitment to the feminist agenda—expanding child care, providing toll-free domestic abuse hot lines, supporting the Family and Medical Leave Act, and above all, backing abortion on demand. Nina Burleigh, who covered the White House for *Time* magazine, described her feelings about Mr. Clinton this way: "I'd be happy to give him [oral sex] just to thank him for keeping abortion legal."

Feminists are quite open about all this. When it comes to supporting President Clinton against credible charges of sexual harassment, some (like Anita Hill) concede that they are operating according to a blatant double standard. To others, if wrongdoing occurred, "I simply don't care" (Betty Friedan) or we should "close [our] eyes" (Anne Roiphe). Call it breathtaking hypocrisy, or call it a sellout of principle, but so speaks the sisterhood.

Feminist support for Bill Clinton demonstrates why one strong argument against utilitarianism is its limited utility. By showing themselves to be intellectually dishonest and unserious, feminists have not only destroyed whatever credibility they once had, they have given a very public, very green light to sexual predators. A few honest feminists have pointed this out. But they are rare exceptions. Most, by essentially blessing the sexual exploitation of women as long as it is done by a powerful man who holds the "correct" views, seem to be fulfilling the worst anti-feminist caricatures.

For others, the cause is the general political viability of the president. Their reasoning goes something like this: the president is an extraordinary leader, and his continuance in office is synonymous with the public good; therefore, unsavory means may be appropriate in the service of that end. This is exactly the argument used in defense of the Nixon administration, and it is as faulty now as it was then.

"The ends justify the means" translates into tossing aside standards in exchange for achieving a cherished ideological or political goal. But who is to decide on behalf of which goals we are to permit unethical (or even illegal) means to be used? Abortion on demand? What about those who want to *restrict* all abortions? Do we give them a free pass to bomb abortion clinics on grounds that they are achieving what they believe to be a greater good? What about a police officer who wants to beat a suspect in order to elicit a confession? What about breaking into a psychiatrist's office and stealing files in order to smear a political opponent? Does it matter if the political opponent is a liberal or a conservative? What about a chief executive who sexually harasses women but happens to be spearheading legislation that would fund Planned Parenthood? What about a chief executive who sexually harasses women and wants to eliminate federal funding for Planned Parenthood? Who arbitrates which ends allow the invocation of a glaring double standard, or even an exemption from the law? Where does it end?*

According to the former Nixon White House operative G. Gordon Liddy, "If the . . . Watergate operation had succeeded, we were going to go that weekend to [Democratic presidential candidate George] McGovern's headquarters and do the same thing. . . . We had a flow chart for the implementation of the plan, and we would have followed it right through the operations in Miami, after the Democrats had selected their candidate." Liddy's justification? "The alternative to Nixon was President McGovern. I would have done a hell of a lot to stop that."

Americans should strongly dissent from these sentiments. Nixonian ethics are wrong because moral precepts are real; they are not like warm candle wax, easily shaped to fit the ends of this or that president, or this or that cause. We do not—at least, we

---

*Of course there are instances when certain ends justify what would otherwise be excessive means. But we reject *prima facie* the use of unlawful or unethical means, and demand compelling justification for exceptions. For an example, see Article I of the Constitution, which guarantees that the writ of habeas corpus may not be suspended, "unless when in cases of rebellion or invasion the public safety may require it." A second example would be participating in an assassination plot against Hitler. A third would be lying in order to save the life of an innocent man. There are commonsense exceptions to the rule, as there are to virtually all rules. But these exceptions are rare, extreme, and apply only when the morality of the end is so enormous (i.e., the survival of a nation or saving the life of an innocent person) that it supersedes the prohibition against excessive means. Obviously this does not apply in this case.

should not—subscribe to the notion that laws apply only to presidents (or causes) we disagree with, but can be suspended for those with whom we agree.

The founders understood all of this quite well; they knew the self-evident superiority of institutions where means are congruent with ends, and their study of history also taught them the importance of prudential means, and ends, as a way of resisting tyranny. Most often, means and ends are inextricably intertwined; indeed, the American Constitution is overwhelmingly a document about the proper procedural means (checks and balances and separation of powers) needed to secure worthy ends (establishing justice, insuring domestic tranquillity, securing the blessings of liberty).

The brand of politics being practiced and advocated by Clinton apologists is based on no code of conduct, no reliable way of deciding what is within or without the bounds of proper political discourse and conduct. The underlying premise is that there are no moral facts, thus reducing politics to what the philosopher Friedrich Nietzsche called (approvingly) the Will to Power. In such a world one cannot make appeals to moral principles; what matters is who controls the levers. Once you leave principle behind, however, you in fact are willing the strong to power—and the strong may not necessarily be on your side, or sympathetic to your dissent.

If narrow (values-free) utilitarian arguments prevail, we will inherit a world in which it will be commonplace to punish people according to the politics they champion rather than the laws they violate or the personal misconduct in which they engage. We will, in short, become a nation of men and not of laws.

V

Finally, what are we to make of the increasingly widespread view that "they all do it"—that politicians are so corrupt they will do anything, from lying to the public, to lying under oath, to obstructing justice, to other high crimes and misdemeanors? Bill Clinton, the argument goes, is typical. No better, no worse.

As it happens, despite what much of the public might think, they all *don't* do it. Most presidents do not commit illegal acts, or lie under oath, or thumb their noses at the law. Most presidents do not chronically deceive, delay, obfuscate, and stonewall federal investigators. This does not mean they are perfect or near perfect; it means merely that most live up to their oath to execute faithfully the laws of the land, and behave in at least a reasonably responsible way. The same is true of most political figures in the nation's capital. Washington, D.C., is not, in fact, a den of thieves, or a house of knaves.

Nor have most Americans really thought so, at least until very recently, else they would *never* have reacted with outrage when presidents are corrupt or violate their oath of office. We need only go back a quarter-century for an example. During an August 22, 1973, press conference, Richard Nixon was asked, "If you were serving in Congress, would you not be considering impeachment proceedings and discussing impeachment possibility against an elected public official who had violated his oath of office?"

In response President Nixon said: "I should . . . point out to you that in the three Kennedy years and the three Johnson years through 1966 when burglarizing of this type did take place, when it was authorized, on a very large scale there was no talk of impeachment and it was quite well known. I should also like to point out that when you ladies and gentlemen indicate your great interest in wiretaps and I understand that the height of the wiretaps was when Robert Kennedy was Attorney General in 1963. I don't criticize him, however. He had over 250 in 1963 and of course the average in the Eisenhower Administration and the Nixon Administration is about 110."

In other words, Mr. Nixon was saying (to quote Robert Kuttner's proverbial taxi driver), "They all do it. What do you expect of politicians? I am no worse than my predecessors." But when we found out about President Nixon's part in an illegal cover-up, we (the courts, Congress, the media, and the public) acted in the national interest—and so, in the end, did he by resigning. The taxi driver's premise was incorrect. In a self-governing and law-abiding nation, we must never allow ourselves to be lulled into passive disgust or indifference, the civic equivalent of a shrug of the shoulders. We must never lose our sense, when appropriate, of outrage.

VI

Bill Clinton certainly did not create political cynicism, though he appears to be its beneficiary. Still, among the most serious repercussions of the denouement of the Clinton scandals will be the damage inflicted on the political profession. And in particular, I should think, upon the Democratic party, of which I was a member until 1986.

In scandals such as this, it is *always* members of the president's party who have particular leverage, and therefore who have a particular responsibility, to hold the president accountable for his actions. During the long months of this scandal, one of my deep disappointments has been the silence of thoughtful Democrats— people whom I know, and like, and have learned from over the years. They are not party hacks, but men of good character. They, too, are troubled by the credible allegations of ethical and criminal wrongdoing. They see the harm that is being inflicted on America. But for month after month they have not said so forcefully, unambiguously, publicly. No Democrat went to the president of the United States and insisted, emphatically, that he do what is right, none insisted that he fully answer questions, stop stonewalling, and come out, immediately, with all of the facts, wherever they might lead. This is shameful.

Throughout this book I have made many analogies to Watergate. But there is one notable *dis*analogy: the absence in the Democratic party of a man like Tennessee Republican Howard Baker, who famously asked of Republican President Richard Nixon: "What did the president know, and when did he know it?" Perhaps Senator Baker's example in Watergate will stiffen some spines. And perhaps then one Democrat will come forward and speak to the president, and remind him of his duties—and in so doing, that Democrat will demonstrate his love for the presidency, and his country, and justice.

Even before the Lewinsky scandal came to light, the political class had come to be viewed with deep contempt. One can cite endless polls showing a decades-long decline in public trust of politicians and political institutions. According to a Pew Research Center report issued earlier this year, over two-thirds of Americans give a fair or poor rating to the ethical and moral practices of federal officials.

Some of this is understandable. Politics has been drained of respect for many reasons: harmful and wasteful government programs, cynical media, election-year "attack ads," criminal convictions of political figures, well-publicized sex scandals, the advent of the independent counsel act (which I discuss in the next chapter), and two defining political events: the Vietnam War and Watergate. An accumulation of individual acts of corruption is marshaled to make a broad institutional indictment.

Some of this indictment has issued out of the ranks of American conservatism, the dominant political movement of the last two decades. A number of well-known conservative figures have engaged in a relentless, uncalibrated assault on Washington and its political institutions. For years, while traveling around the country giving speeches, I, too, took the obligatory shots at Washington. Some were justified. But some weren't. I found out that you can say virtually anything derogatory about Washington and elicit nods of approval, or laughs, or even applause.

I still believe criticism of Washington is warranted, and that much of what the government does is counterproductive and meddlesome. Among those who practice politics, there are more than enough examples of conflicts of interest; abuse of power; narrow partisanship; intellectual atrophy; an absence of candor and courtesy; scandal; and lack of courage. But I am more careful in what I say, and how I say it. Unremittingly hostile anti-political sentiments are corrosive and unwarranted. Legitimate anger at politics needs to be more selective, more focused, more exact.

Most Americans would be surprised to learn that, in general, politics today is *less* corrupt than perhaps at any point in American history. But it is, and for reasons largely having to do with political reforms, disclosure rules, a more aggressive press, the passing away of Tammany Hall–like political machines and party "bosses." According to the scholar Norman Ornstein, federal politics is much cleaner today than it has been throughout most of American history.

Because of the flaws of human nature, the problems with politics will always be with us. But we need to maintain both historical perspective and fair judgment. In my own experience in Washington I have found plenty of honorable people, on both sides of the aisle: devoted people who perform their jobs in an ethical and upright manner, and who give the lie to any cynical generalization about politicians. For the obvious reasons, you almost never hear about this encouraging side of the capital.

We—and by "we" I mean in the first instance the political class itself—need to reclaim some of the high purpose of politics. Statecraft is not simply about spending bills, subcommittee hearings, and continuing resolutions. In a jaded world, we need to remind the public, by word and deed, that politics is also, and importantly, about efforts to achieve justice, ensure human dignity and the rule of law, and strive for the good society.

In his elegant autobiography *Pilgrim's Way,* the late novelist and Member of Parliament John Buchan wrote that public life is "the worthiest ambition. Politics is still the greatest and the most honourable adventure." So it was, and so it still can be. Unfortunately, many people now believe the opposite. Those who feed this belief and foster more cynicism in the people are acting shamefully. Among their number—indeed most prominent among them—is the president of the United States.

Chapter 4

Ken Starr

Defense of President Clinton: *Historically, almost all Democratic party leaders have been strong advocates of the independent counsel law. Reflecting this sentiment, President Clinton reauthorized the law in 1994. But recent events have caused many Democrats and liberals to become deeply disenchanted with the statute. Former White House counsel Lanny Davis said earlier this year that he believes "this independent counsel statute should be eliminated. It's been abused. It's a serious problem in our American system, and we need to get rid of it." Jeffrey Toobin, a prosecutor in the Office of Independent Counsel under Lawrence Walsh (who investigated Iran-contra), now writes about the "perversity of the independent-counsel law in action." And House Minority Leader Richard Gephardt recently said of the independent counsel law, "it's not working at all well, and we ought to change the law, limit an independent counsel to one particular fact situation, get it done in a meaningful time, and let's move on."*

According to the president's defenders, the most compelling case against the independent counsel statute can be summed up in two words: Ken Starr. To an unprecedented degree, they aver, he is unaccountable, uncontrollable, and a destructive force in American politics. James Carville puts it this way: "We have an out-of-control sex-crazed person that is running the [investigation], has spent $40 million of taxpayers' money investigating people's sex lives."

Judge Starr is accused of being exceedingly partisan and political. According to Hillary Clinton, "We get a politically motivated prosecutor who is allied with the right-wing opponents of my husband, who has literally spent four years looking . . . at every telephone call we've made, every check we've ever written, scratching for dirt, intimidating witnesses, doing everything possible to try to make some accusation against my husband." Specific complaints and/or charges include the fact that Judge Starr represents tobacco companies; spoke at the Regent University Law School, whose founder is Pat Robertson; announced he would accept (but later withdrew from) a deanship of the Schools of Law and Public Policy at Pepperdine University, which is funded in part by Richard Mellon Scaife, a philanthropist who supports conservative causes and movements—including ones critical of the president; and (according to apologists for the president) has leaked improper information to the press. Because Mr. Starr is a Republican, Clinton adviser Rahm Emanuel complained to CNN's Larry King, "You don't have the referee come from the other team."

A charge frequently leveled against Judge Starr is that he is delaying the investigation. According to Mr. Gephardt, "I think he's been at this for four years. He spent $40 million. I think any objective observer could say, when is he going to bring this to an end? I mean, how long does this go on?" In April, Lanny Davis urged Mr. Starr to "give us a reasonable terminable point to what has been an interminable $40 million investigation."

Still another charge is that Judge Starr, in the words of Mr. Davis, is "undermining the very integrity of the criminal justice system." Clinton advocates charge him with prosecutorial abuse for, among other things, issuing subpoenas to Monica Lewinsky's mother and to White House aide Sidney Blumenthal, and demanding sales receipts of books Ms. Lewinsky purchased at local Washington, D.C., stores.

To the Clinton team, Ken Starr's tactics are "frightening" and "absurd," "vicious" and "lawless." His investigation is an "inquisition"; it "smacks of Gestapo" and "outstrips McCarthyism." Starr is "scary," a "spineless, gutless weasel," and "engaged in an anti-constitutional destructiveness." He uses the "instruments of intimidation and smear without restraint." And the office of independent counsel is filled with "a crew of prosecutorial pirates." Starr himself is a "thug"; a "zealot"; a "Grand Inquisitor for life"; "Captain Ahab"; "on a vendetta"; acting out of "personal temper tantrums." He is a "sex-obsessed independent counsel" engaged in a "slimy, scuzzy, little sleazy sex investigation"; a "sex-obsessed person who's out to get the president"; a "real Nixonian character"; a person trying to "chill people's constitutional rights"; and a man who is "unfair" and has "lost all sense of reason, proportionality, and perspective." He is a "hell-bent prosecutor who shows no limits in judgment or willingness to prosecute in the sense of proportionality"; "in danger of prosecutorial misconduct"; acting "irresponsibly, illegally"; and should "go jump in a lake."

Response

The core of this particular defense is, first, that the independent counsel law is a bad one that is doing damage to our political culture; second, that Judge Starr in particular is a partisan,

right-wing, irresponsible federal prosecutor whose sole aim is
to bring down President Clinton, by whatever means necessary;
and, finally, that whatever report is issued to Congress will be
fatally flawed because of the irresponsible conduct of its author.

I believe the first assertion is right, but the second and third
are wrong.

I

The independent counsel law was passed by Congress in 1978
as part of the Watergate-inspired Ethics in Government Act. It
allowed for the appointment of a "special prosecutor" to investigate suspected crimes by high-ranking executive branch officials.
It was reenacted (with minor changes) in 1982, when the formal
title of the office was changed from "special prosecutor" to "independent counsel," and again in 1987. Although the Reagan
administration argued that the law was unconstitutional, in June
1988 the Supreme Court upheld its constitutionality. The law,
which must be renewed every five years, died in 1992 because of
Republican opposition, but in 1994 President Clinton signed a
bill restoring it.

The law requires that the attorney general, whenever he or she
receives specific, credible evidence of possible crimes by high-
ranking executive branch officials, conduct a preliminary investigation. If after ninety days "reasonable grounds" exist to warrant
further investigation, the attorney general must apply to the court
for the appointment (by a special three-judge panel) of an independent counsel. The independent counsel's mandate, as specifically fashioned by the judicial panel, is to investigate and, if
appropriate, prosecute. The attorney general may remove an independent counsel from office for "good cause," but that decision is
subject to judicial review.

During the 1980s, proponents of the independent counsel law said the law was constitutional, and the Supreme Court agreed. In the majority opinion, Chief Justice William Rehnquist argued that the act did not violate the principle of the separation of powers by "impermissibly interfer[ing] . . ." with the functions of the executive branch, even though "it is undeniable that the act reduces the amount of control or supervision that the attorney general and, through him, the president exercises over the investigation and prosecution of a certain class of alleged criminal activity."

The ruling was embraced because, it was contended, an administration cannot be expected to investigate wrongdoing by its own high-ranking members. In order to ensure a fair, comprehensive investigation, the power to prosecute had to be insulated from the president. The law would thus avoid inherent conflicts of interest, and also guard against governmental abuse of power. The result would be to "depoliticize the power to prosecute" (in the words of the *Washington Post*), ensure integrity, and increase public confidence in government.

I reject these arguments. I was, and despite the Supreme Court's ruling I remain, a critic of the independent counsel law, above all because I believe it undercuts one of the framers' first principles: the separation of powers. The Constitution specifies (in Article II, Section I) that executive power must be under the control of the president. Nobody—not even the Supreme Court majority who upheld the statute—disputes that the functions performed by the independent counsel are executive. And nobody disputes that the independent counsel act reduces the amount of control the president (via the attorney general) exercises over the investigation. Granting the independent counsel power over federal prosecutions outside the control of the chief executive—which is the very goal of the statute—is, I believe, a violation of the Constitution. Throughout most of American history, including through Watergate, the abuse of executive power was checked by other branches of government (e.g., congressional investigations and impeachment), and by public accountability (e.g., voting people out of office).

But even apart from the constitutional issue, there are other problems with the statute. It absolves Congress partially of one of its most important duties: scrutiny of the executive branch. The independent counsel is for all intents and purposes accountable to no one. There is no way effectively to check bias, prejudice, and tendentiousness within the office of independent counsel. The independent counsel has an almost unlimited budget. He has extraordinary prosecutorial power. He has only one target, and all the incentives are to find that target guilty of a crime.

In his powerful dissent in the independent counsel case, Justice Antonin Scalia said this: "How frightening it must be to have your own independent counsel and staff appointed, with nothing else to do but to investigate you until investigation is no longer worthwhile—with whether it is worthwhile not depending upon what such judgments usually hinge on, competing responsibilities. And to have that counsel and staff decide, with no basis for comparison, whether what you have done is bad enough, willful enough, and provable enough, to warrant an indictment. How admirable the constitutional system that provides the means to avoid such a distortion. And how unfortunate the judicial decision that has permitted it."

Note well, however: it is a logical fallacy to assume that, because the independent counsel law might be used unfairly against innocent people, everyone who has been pursued by an independent counsel is innocent. Clearly, some targets of investigation are people who violated the law.

Moreover, the statute, whatever its shortcomings, has been ruled constitutional by the highest court in the land. There is an obligation to comply with it, and thanks to President Clinton's signature, it is the law of the land. One of the most passionate defenders of reauthorization was President Clinton himself; he dismissed Republicans who considered it to be constitutionally suspect, a potential tool of partisan attack, and a waste of taxpayer money. In fact, the president said, "the independent counsel statute has been in the past and is today a force for government integrity and public confidence." He called the bill "good for the American people and good for their confidence in democracy." The irony is that, four years later, he is doing all he can to subvert the good-government law he championed.

II

What cannot go uncommented upon is the stunning hypocrisy on the issue of the independent counsel law. In 1998 Anthony Lewis of the *New York Times* quoted at length, and quite favorably, from an article in *The American Prospect* by University of Chicago professor Cass Sunstein, calling for the repeal of the law or for allowing it to die without renewal. Mr. Lewis drew attention to the act's "fundamental problem," which is that more and more emphasis will be placed on "prosecuting high officials and less on solving the country's substantive problems."

But flash back to 1987, when the same Anthony Lewis was among the independent counsel act's biggest cheerleaders. Then, the law was a civic necessity. Mr. Lewis dismissed as "frivolous" the arguments by the Reagan Justice Department that the law was unconstitutional, insisting passionately that the law worked "as a credible way to clear wrongly accused officials," whereas killing it would "let Presidents and Attorneys General control investigations of themselves and their colleagues." As to why the Reagan Justice Department was eager to do away with the law, "my guess," Lewis wrote, "is a simple one: Officials are afraid now of what Judge Walsh [Lawrence Walsh, the Iran-contra independent counsel] and other independent counsels are doing."

In another column from the late 1980s Lewis chided critics of the statute for using arguments "far removed from precedent and reason." And in yet another column, he referred to the law as "a common-sensical response to an urgent problem of governance." As for the contention that the independent counsel would infringe on the president's constitutional power, that was part of a "strident public campaign" by the "radical right in this country." And the Supreme Court's 1988 decision to uphold the law? "No decision in recent terms of the Court," Mr. Lewis wrote in hailing it, "has had deeper implications for the American system of government."

So what accounts for the change? My guess is a simple one: in the late 1980s, the objects of independent counsel investigations were members of the Reagan administration. In the late 1990s, the object of independent counsel investigation is Bill Clinton.

Anthony Lewis is hardly alone. When the Supreme Court upheld the statute in 1988, journalist Haynes Johnson welcomed "a great decision, an affirmation of the integrity of the American political system." He added that the decision, which left the "right wing collectively gnashing its teeth," was "philosophically . . . in keeping with the tradition that constitutional checks and balances were created to guard against governmental abuses of power."

But in 1998, Mr. Johnson told PBS's Jim Lehrer, "All of a sudden we're investigating acts that took place twenty years ago that were not about the acts of a sitting president. We're investigating sexual allegations that may not even be a federal crime, or a crime at all perhaps. And so these things seem to expand and grow and grow like amoebas, and I think there is a real problem about reining in the old American tradition of reining in power." Mr. Johnson now considers the law something less than "an affirmation of the integrity of the American political system." Now it's an outright threat, and we need to "radically shrink the power of this act."

Lloyd Cutler, a former counsel to President Clinton, has said, "I testified in favor of the law when it was passed. . . . But I've finally come around to thinking the cure is worse than the disease. Under this system, some of the independent counsels have become men on

horseback. They turn it into a game of gotcha, and it just goes on forever." Here is yet one more example of Clinton-era enlightenment.

In his book *Opening Arguments*, Jeffrey Toobin laments the
abuses of the office, admitting he joined the Iran-contra investigation because he was looking for a "crusade." His quarry was
Elliott Abrams, President Reagan's assistant secretary of state for
inter-American affairs, whom Mr. Toobin investigated with
what he called "an enthusiasm that bordered on the unseemly."
Mr. Toobin now writes that "we had nothing less than a blank
check to uncover and rectify the misdeeds of a corrupt and dis-
honorable administration."

One ought not begrudge others the right to change their mind;
often, new facts and circumstances persuade people to rethink
previously held, even deeply held, positions. That can be to the
good. But these vast shifts in opinion do not seem a consequence of
studied reflection, particularly since the tactics employed by the
independent counsel today are arguably less aggressive than those
employed by Judge Walsh in the 1980s. To put it another way: when
it was members of the Reagan administration who were being tar-
geted, people defending the independent counsel act invoked high-
minded civic principle. Now that the target is a president to whom
they are politically and ideologically sympathetic, we suddenly
hear worries about prosecutorial overreach; calls for reining in the
law; and appeals to eliminate it completely.

President Clinton's defenders charge that the opposite hypocrisy
obtains among conservatives. It was they, after all, who made the
strongest arguments against the independent counsel law during
the 1980s, but pointedly refrain from criticizing the statute now
that Ken Starr is investigating President Clinton. Conservatives,
say the president's apologists, are now enjoying payback, big-time.

Some of this criticism is warranted; the Republican criticisms
of the independent counsel law are not nearly as passionate as
they were a decade ago. Still, most conservative legal scholars

have remained consistent in their views. And to their credit, when the issue of reauthorization of the independent counsel law came up in 1994—during the Clinton administration—many conservatives and Republicans urged the president to allow it to expire. While just over half of all Republicans in the Senate voted for reauthorization, a solid majority of Republicans in the House, usually considered the more partisan of the two legislative bodies, voted against reauthorization. If the major aim of conservative Republicans was to do damage to the Clinton administration via the independent counsel statute, then they should have urged passage of the law. In fact, many did not.

III

Former proponents of the independent counsel act often claim that it worked well enough until the power of the office linked up with one Kenneth Starr. In this scenario, not the statute but Judge Starr is the problem: an irresponsibly aggressive, sex-obsessed, right-wing zealot who to an unprecedented degree has abused the power of his office.

In fact, Starr is a man whose professional career—including stints on the United States Court of Appeals for the District of Columbia and as solicitor general in the administration of George Bush—has been characterized by sobriety, probity, judiciousness, and personal and professional integrity. This description comes from people on both sides of the political spectrum.

Former Clinton White House counsel Abner Mikva called Starr "a person of integrity." *The New Yorker*'s Toobin quotes a former Justice Department colleague of Starr's as saying, "Ken is not on the Supreme Court today because he was viewed as suspect by the Republican right. They called him a squish—too moderate and open-minded."

In 1993 the Senate Ethics Committee—split evenly between Democrats and Republicans—investigated sexual misconduct charges against Oregon Republican Senator Robert Packwood. When the committee needed a discreet and impartial arbiter to determine which parts of Senator Packwood's diaries were relevant to the case and which should remain private and protected, Judge Starr was chosen for the job. According to the *Washington Post*, "even those who regularly crossed swords with him credited him with being fair. He was not seen as ideologically driven." So confident were the committee members in Starr's fairness that they waived the right to appeal his decisions.

Said Walter Dellinger, then head of the Office of Legal Counsel at the Clinton Justice Department, "I have known Ken Starr since he was one of my students at Duke Law School, and I've always known him to be a fair-minded person." Here is Arthur Spitzer, legal director of the American Civil Liberties Union: "If I was going to be the subject of an investigation, I would rather have him [Starr] investigate me than almost anyone I can think of." And four former attorneys general, including Griffin Bell, who served in the Jimmy Carter administration, signed a letter testifying: "We know Mr. Starr to be an individual of highest personal and professional integrity," one who has "exhibited exemplary judgment and commitment to the highest ethical standards and the rule of law."

Well, say Clinton defenders, perhaps at one time Judge Starr was a fair man, but now he has become a prosecutorial Frankenstein. As evidence, they cite his tactics. In fact, however, Judge Starr has not done anything monstrous; if he had, the president (through his attorney general, Janet Reno) could fire him for cause. Indeed, if Judge Starr were guilty of half of what the Clinton loyalists have accused him, Attorney General Reno should fire him. But that is unlikely to happen, since Judge Starr appears to have followed proper prosecutorial procedures. If evidence ever came to light that he engaged in improper activities, he should of course be reprimanded.

Former Reagan Deputy Attorney General Arnold I. Burns points out that the "hardball tactics" the media and general public are now seeing up close "are not only 'by the book,' but actually reflect greater restraint than the actions of many prosecutors around the country." It is also worth noting that Judge Starr's ethics counsel is the widely respected Samuel Dash, who was the Democratic majority's chief counsel during Watergate and the drafter of the independent counsel statute.

As a helpful reference point, consider the prosecution tactics employed during the Iran-contra investigation, when independent counsel Lawrence Walsh called before the grand jury Colonel Oliver North's wife, minister, and lawyer*—tactics far more legally questionable than what Starr did in calling before the grand jury Monica Lewinsky's mother and Clinton acolyte Sidney Blumenthal. At the time, there was no outcry from the media condemning Judge Walsh's "zealous" or "partisan" tactics—not even when he indicted former Defense Secretary Caspar Weinberger just days before the 1992 election. For the most part, Lawrence Walsh was treated, as was Archibald Cox before him, with deference and respect.

Ken Starr is "sex-obsessed," claims James Carville, obsessively. The Clinton public relations offensive portrays Starr as a religious fanatic—a prudish, self-righteous, uptight figure straight out of a novel by Nathaniel Hawthorne. This helps explain the sneering comments by senior presidential aide Sidney Blumenthal, who, speaking at Harvard, referred to Judge Starr's deputy Hickman Ewing as a "religious fanatic" and to Starr as "Grand

---

*Colonel North's baby-sitter was subpoenaed but, as she was sixteen years old and in California, they did not bring her before the grand jury, though she was interviewed.

Inquisitor for life" and a "zealot on a mission divined from a higher authority." What qualifies Ewing to be called a "religious fanatic"? Three offenses. He prays daily; he attends an evangelical church regularly; and he doesn't drink.

Carville and Blumenthal's "tactics" are unprecedented ad hominem attacks against an officer of the court. They are transparently bigoted. And they are also baseless. There is no evidence for the charge of a "sex obsession," and Carville has never offered any. Call it a Big Lie. Or call it the Clinton Defense.

What about the Starr investigation itself, which the president's men consider a "sexual inquisition"? As I demonstrate in greater detail in the first chapter, Judge Starr's investigation—authorized by Clinton Attorney General Janet Reno—is not an investigation into the president's sex life; it is an investigation of credible allegations of perjury and obstruction of justice. It happens that the crimes being investigated were likely committed in an attempt to cover up the president's infidelity, but the key words are "criminal cover-up," not "infidelity." Sexual infidelity alone would never have been investigated in the first place—and if such an attempt were ever made, it would not have received the approval of the attorney general or the three-judge panel.

Stuart Taylor, a former *New York Times* legal reporter and now a columnist with *National Journal,* posed to a number of current and former high-level Clinton appointees the question: what should Ken Starr have done once he was presented with Linda Tripp's story and Monica Lewinsky's statements on tape. According to Mr. Taylor, "They all said that—even though perjury is rarely prosecuted in civil cases—Tripp's allegations warranted aggressive criminal investigation, and that the wiring of Tripp to seek more taped evidence from Lewinsky was justified."

Orwell once said that sometimes the first duty of a responsible man is to restate the obvious. So let us here restate the obvious: the independent counsel has a legal obligation to pursue credible charges of criminal conduct. The fact that these criminal allegations are interwined with sexual misconduct—the reason there is a sexual component to this case in the first place—has nothing to do with Ken Starr. It has everything to do with Bill Clinton. The president is responsible for dragging us through this tawdry spectacle. It was he who, by his own action, dictated the context for this part of the investigation.

Mrs. Clinton charges that the independent counsel is "politically motivated," and Rahm Emanuel complains that when it comes to special prosecutors and independent counsels, "you don't have the referee come from the other team." They might be interested to learn (or, in Mrs. Clinton's case, to be reminded) that Archibald Cox, the special prosecutor in the Nixon-era Watergate scandal, was a Democrat, a Harvard professor, solicitor general in the Kennedy administration, and a close friend of the Kennedy family. For his Watergate special prosecution force, Cox recruited a number of former Kennedy aides. Richard Nixon was later to write that "if [Attorney General–Designate Elliot] Richardson had searched specifically for the man whom I would have least trusted . . . he could hardly have done better" than Cox.

Former Nixon Attorney General Richard Kleindienst said, "Archibald Cox is one of the brightest and most gifted lawyers in the country, but he was also one of the most articulate spokesmen for the liberal wing of the Democratic Party. He had been very much involved in Jack Kennedy's campaign in 1960—that is not the characteristic of an impartial special prosecutor. It was doomed to failure from the very outset because Archie Cox expanded his perceived function and role, far beyond the Watergate situation, so that it turned out to be a special prosecution of the Nixon administration, generally speaking. Nobody ever contemplated that. You can't have that kind of a person in that kind of office under those circumstances."

President Nixon fired Mr. Cox, but was forced by public opinion to replace him. As Nixon's chief of staff Alexander Haig later wrote, "Whoever the appointee turned out to be, and whatever his other qualifications were, he had to be a Democrat." Which he was (Leon Jaworski).

Now, that an independent counsel (or special prosecutor) may be "political"—that is, he has political views, even strong ones—does not invalidate an investigation. In Washington—and indeed, beyond Washington—it turns out that most people are "political"; that is, they bring to their work a certain view of the world. That fact in and of itself does not taint an investigation. That Archibald Cox was a liberal Democrat does not mean that the crimes of Watergate did not happen; or should not have been investigated; or should not have been investigated by Archibald Cox. What matter are not political motivations but objective facts. Political motivations become relevant only when they substitute themselves for the facts of the case.

Then there is the charge leveled against Judge Starr that he is responsible for slowing the investigation. But Judge Starr's investigation has been expanded four times at the request of, or with the approval of, Clinton Attorney General Janet Reno. His mandate keeps enlarging, and the length of the investigation increasing, because the web of deceit is so massive. But the real reason Judge Starr cannot give a "reasonable terminable point" to what has been an "interminable investigation" is simple: the stonewalling and delaying tactics of the Clinton administration.

These tactics (like the attack on the independent counsel) are unprecedented—even by Watergate standards. President Clinton has refused to cooperate personally with the Starr investigation, after promising he would do so. His administration has invoked attorney-client and executive privileges to prevent aides from testifying. It invented the "protective function privilege," which would, in the words of a federal appeals court decision, prohibit

Secret Service testimony even in cases where evidence, viewed in the light of subsequent events, would supply a key element in the proof of a serious crime. And it has resisted a "fast track" to the Supreme Court to decide expeditiously the matter of government-paid, attorney-client privilege.

What we are seeing is the political equivalent of the four-corners stall, perfected by former North Carolina Tarheel basketball coach Dean Smith. Hold the ball. Run out the clock. And wait for your opponents to make mistakes. The difference is that Coach Smith never tried to present the four-corners stall as a "hurry-up offense." Nor did he ever blame the other team for slowing down the game.

Why, then, does Judge Starr engender deep mistrust among the public (according to one poll, only 22 percent of Americans profess "a lot of confidence" that Kenneth Starr's report on President Clinton will be "fair and impartial")? Why is so much anger directed against an independent counsel fulfilling his responsibility (even imperfectly) rather than at a president brazenly shirking his? Part of the explanation lies in Starr's own missteps. His acceptance of a job at Pepperdine before the completion of his investigation (a job from which he subsequently withdrew) was inadvisable. Upon taking the post of independent counsel, it would have been prudent to drop all his outside legal work. His on-the-record interview with a hostile and tendentious editor of a new media magazine was foolish. And he waited too long to present a series of thoughtful speeches that put his investigation in context.

Still, almost all Judge Starr's faults have to do with lapses of political judgment and a certain tone-deafness. When it comes to public relations, the *New York Times* has called him a "one-man train wreck," but the same *New York Times* puts these shortcomings in proper perspective: "Nothing Mr. Starr has done excuses the campaign of vilification conducted by the Clintons and their televised mouthpieces. That campaign is designed to deny Mr. Starr and the taxpayers the benefits of a completed investigation into matters of legal weight about which President and Mrs. Clinton and agencies of the Administration have consistently refused to tell the full truth."

Judge Starr's low popularity is overwhelmingly due to the fact that he is the object of a well orchestrated and relentless smear campaign. University of Illinois law professor Ronald Rotunda, who was an assistant counsel for Democrats on the Senate Watergate Committee, told the *Washington Post* that attacks on Starr's integrity are baseless, and are belied by the fact that Clinton's attorney general, Janet Reno, has continued to assign him new matters to investigate. "This is basically a blatantly political attack," according to Professor Rotunda. Even some Democrats are unnerved by the scorched-earth tactics of James Carville. When asked about Carville's plan to mount an aggressive public campaign against the independent counsel, Senator Daniel Patrick Moynihan said, "Nonsense. [Starr] is appointed. He has his responsibilities. Let him carry them out."

But they won't allow it, for there is cold utility to the Clinton war on an officer of the court: it appears to be working. The truth is that any person investigating this president would be on the receiving end of slashing attacks by Clinton loyalists. Their tactics have been perfected, and rewarded, over time. It is what they know, and how they play, and what they do. They have indeed turned much of the White House into a War Room.

Indeed, the president's apologists have been candid about what James Carville himself calls a "war." One White House official has dubbed it "our continuing campaign to destroy Ken Starr." A White House that views politics as something akin to war is an alarming matter. It implicitly means that warlike (read: extra-constitutional) tactics are justifiable, if necessary.

Charles Colson, a top Nixon aide who has since become a committed Christian, explains the Nixon White House's mind-set this way: "We used to look at politics as warfare: Democrats and Republicans; liberals and conservatives. Nixon had been badly treated when he was out of office. We had believed at the time—and later had good evidence—that our campaign plane in 1968 was bugged. We knew that the IRS had come after a lot of our friends in the Kennedy-Johnson years. It was the IRS issue that made Watergate explode: we felt we were in a war, and now that we were in power, we were going to use that leverage. When Nixon was elected, the *Washington Post* had an article saying that Nixon's coming to Washington will be like Hitler's coming to Paris; we didn't feel very welcome. It was a 'we vs. them' attitude which, probably, to a degree, was exacerbated by Nixon's personality."

The president's defenders use political cynicism to their advantage and reduce everything to "mere politics." Their stated goal is to weaken Judge Starr to the point that, no matter how compelling the evidence he presents, a weary public will dismiss it as "partisan." To achieve this, they know they must make truth subservient to spin, even if it does damage—as it surely will—to government integrity and public confidence in our legal institutions. Such is the Clinton way.

Finally, assume for the sake of the argument that Ken Starr is guilty of all the charges made by Clinton apologists. What does it say about some Clinton defenders that they are reduced to saying, in effect, "No one would ever have found out about the president's transgressions if it weren't for a sex-obsessed, out-of-control prosecutor?" Implicit in this particular defense is the concession that the president did do something wrong, though that bothers them not at all.

Assume, too, that Archibald Cox was guilty of all the charges made by Nixon apologists. Assume that both men were partisan; used overly aggressive prosecutorial tactics; and went well beyond their investigative mandates. Assume both men wanted to "bring down" their respective presidential targets. These facts alone would still not exonerate either president. Complaining about a law you do not like, being carried out by a man whom you do not trust, is no defense.

In both the Nixon and the Clinton cases, the underlying question is the same: were presidential lies followed by attempts to obstruct justice? All the rest is a distraction—a slick attempt to divert public attention from the possible criminal behavior of an American president. In the end, the attacks against Ken Starr, like the attacks against Archibald Cox before him, are a sideshow. Here and now, the conduct of Bill Clinton should be, and finally will be, center stage.

Chapter 5

Law

Defense of President Clinton: *The core of this defense is that the president deserves the benefit of the doubt and the presumption of innocence. On the Lewinsky matter, his defenders assert, "we know very few facts" (Mrs. Clinton), and the facts we do know support the president's version of events.*

In early June Lanny Davis, the former White House special counsel, argued that "there are facts, and there are nonfacts. At the moment we are looking at a bunch of allegations, unsubstantiated innuendo that has caused Ken Starr, I think, to misuse the subpoena power." And White House counsel Jack Quinn assures us, "the president, in fact, has answered the core questions at issue here in the Lewinsky matter. For example, he has said very forcefully to the American people there is no sex involved in that relationship. He did not lie about it. He did not ask anyone else to lie about it."

A second defense is to play down the significance of the charges themselves; in the words of Mr. Davis, "Let's remember what this investigation is about. It's about an alleged false statement in the middle of a civil case, which has been thrown out of court."

A third defense is that because independent counsel Kenneth Starr is out to get the president, Mr. Clinton should effectively invoke his Fifth Amendment right and not address the questions surrounding the Lewinsky scandal. Mr. Davis says that Judge Starr is "hell-bent on destroying him. In those circumstances, it would be foolhardy for [the president] to cooperate in any way with Mr. Starr." With that argument in place, James Carville advances to the next stage: "If there is a privilege that [President Clinton] can assert under the law, given the behavior of Mr. Starr and his henchmen, then he ought to assert that privilege and clearly executive privilege and the attorney-client privilege. . . . If there's a Fifth Amendment right the president can assert, I think he ought to assert that because these people have gone around and subpoenaed mothers, they've subpoenaed bookstores, they've subpoenaed people to talk about conversations with reporters."

A fourth defense is to counsel patience and argue that this is only a legal (as opposed to a civic) matter. We should wait until everything is to be settled in a court of law. The Reverend Jesse Jackson put it this way: "This matter of the trial should be handled by lawyers, and I would simply urge the entire public to deal with this matter more in a courtroom than a newsroom and more with judges than journalists. . . . Let's face the facts as they are and be patient in democracy."

Response

This defense rests on the assumption that the Clintons want to get to the bottom of the allegations in the Lewinsky scandal, but we (and they) know too few facts; the facts we do know tend to exonerate the president; and even if the president did lie under oath, the nature and facts of the civil case itself excuse him of any wrongdoing. The president, who has emphatically denied the charges against him, for many months effectively invoked his Fifth Amendment right against self-incrimination only because he has to protect himself against an independent counsel who wants to destroy him; and because these are legal matters, we should wait patiently for the courts to decide on the president's guilt or innocence. That is the American way.

I take issue with each of these arguments.

I

During Mrs. Clinton's televised floating of the charge of a "vast right-wing conspiracy," she also insisted that she was intensely interested in what the facts are, but that "we know very few facts right now." Until all the facts come out, she added, "I don't think it's fruitful at all to speculate or to engage in hypotheticals." What matters, she concluded, was that her husband not become "distracted," lest he be prevented from "work[ing] very hard every day" in order to "help our people."

There is one very large problem with the first lady's account. As George Will so aptly put it, "The man across from her at the breakfast table surely has lots of pertinent facts right now. So Hillary Clinton might begin to slake her thirst for facts by saying: 'Pass the marmalade, and by the way, is the *New York Times* right that Monica Lewinsky met alone with you late last month, two weeks after being subpoenaed by Paula Jones's lawyers and a week before Lewinsky filed her affidavit saying she had not had sexual relations with you? Help yourself to the bacon, dear, and what *did* you and 'that woman' talk about, other than saving Social Security?'"

Feigned ignorance is then conjoined with subterfuge. When asked why the president would not provide a detailed explanation of his relationship with Ms. Lewinsky, the first lady, an accomplished lawyer and a graduate of the Yale Law School, answered, "Because there's an investigation going on, nobody can expect the president to say anything more publicly, because if there weren't an investigation he could, but because there is an investigation, he can't." She added this: "I hope every American understands that. And I know that must be very frustrating for people. But that is the way the system works."

President Clinton, who also attended Yale Law School, similarly insisted for weeks that the law prohibited him from speaking out. During a press conference the president refrained from commenting on the Lewinsky matter because he was "honoring the rules of the investigation."

The only trouble is that the system doesn't work the way the first lady says it works, and the "rules" of investigation the president says he was "honoring" don't exist. As they both surely know, there are *no* legal restrictions forbidding the president from commenting on the matter; federal laws prohibit only *prosecutors* from commenting on evidence being presented before a grand jury investigation. In early February, the White House was finally forced to concede that the president was not legally prohibited from giving a comprehensive explanation of his relationship with Ms. Lewinsky.

From here we move to the "nonfacts" defense, the goal of which is to persuade the public that the case against the president is built on sand; it is nothing but "unsubstantiated innuendo," vicious rumors, wild accusations. What we know, defenders of the president argue, is that the president has denied, under oath and in public statements, any criminal wrongdoing and any sexual relations with "that woman"; and Monica Lewinsky signed an affidavit denying she had a sexual relationship with the president. And that is about all we are said to know.

But in fact, even *before* Judge Starr issues his final report, we know quite a lot more. We know, for example, that there are at least twenty hours of tape recordings between Ms. Lewinsky and her erstwhile colleague Linda Tripp, in which Ms. Lewinsky goes into detail about her affair with the president, and in which, according to people who have heard the tapes, she claims President Clinton directed her to testify falsely in the Paula Jones case. We know that Ms. Lewinsky's lawyers gave independent counsel Starr a "proffer" of testimony in which Ms. Lewinsky reportedly confirmed a sexual relationship with the president. We know that Ms. Lewinsky told others about her encounters with the president, and that others claim to have heard Mr. Clinton's messages left on Ms. Lewinsky's home answering machine. We know that under oath Ms. Tripp said she was told by Ms. Lewinsky to "lie and deny."

We know the president gave Ms. Lewinsky gifts that have been turned over to investigators, and that she sent courier packages to the president. We know, according to lawyers familiar with Ms. Lewinsky's proffer, that the proffer says the president told Ms. Lewinsky she would not have to turn over the gifts, subpoenaed by Ms. Jones's lawyers, if she did not have them in her possession. We know that Ms. Lewinsky turned the gifts over to Mr. Clinton's personal secretary, Betty Currie, who subsequently gave them to Mr. Starr's investigators.

We know that Ms. Lewinsky, a former intern, made at least thirty-seven visits to the White House after she was reassigned to the Pentagon, and that Mr. Clinton met with her after she was subpoenaed by Ms. Jones's lawyers. We know that Ms. Lewinsky received extensive personal attention and job placement help from Vernon Jordan, a Washington power broker and Clinton confidant. We know that Ms. Lewinsky received a job offer from Revlon after Mr. Jordan personally called Ron Perelman, chairman of Revlon's parent company, on her behalf. We know that Ms. Lewinsky received a job offer from then–U.N. Ambassador Bill Richardson after he personally met with the young woman at the Watergate complex, where she lives. We know that according to Ms. Lewinsky's proffer, as reported in the *New York Times,* Mr. Clinton told her that if she were in New York, she might be able to avoid testifying in the Jones lawsuit. And we know that Ms. Lewinsky's job offers came from New York. And even this long list does not exhaust all we know.

These facts may not be legally dispositive, but they amount to more, much more, than idle rumor, speculation, and mere innuendo. It is true that, in a perfect sense, we don't really know what is in Linda Tripp's testimony, or in the tapes, or in the proffer; it is also true that too much of what has been reported about the various deals that have been proposed, or the physical evidence under investigation, has turned out to be false. Yet the level of certainty being demanded by the president's defenders is comparable to asking that the public find him guilty beyond a shadow of a doubt. That is a standard of "knowing" that is higher than that required even of a trial jury, and, needless to say, the president is not (yet) on trial.

Two more points. First, words like "facts" and "known" and "not known" have both common and legal meanings, and the president's apologists disingenuously decide which to use based on expediency. As a consequence, when reporters ask what the president *knows* (common meaning), his defenders can forthrightly say he *knows* nothing (legal meaning), and therefore neither do we. We should not allow ourselves to be taken in by this.

Second, while we ourselves cannot know, with theological certainty, the truth of the allegations against the president, we are not thereby excused from considering them and making the most plausible judgment we can make about them. The fact that the "innuendo" defense has found such favor among the American people is more an indictment of our timidity than an encomium to our fairness. One doesn't have to subscribe to the belief that "where there's smoke, there's fire" to want to get at the truth about what would otherwise be some pretty unlikely coincidences. To recall the words of the first lady, there are around the White House an awful lot of turtles on fence posts.

As for Jack Quinn's assertion that the president has "very forcefully" provided us with a denial of the charge, that is not true of Mr. Clinton's initial response, which was hesitant, qualified, and unconvincing. On January 21, during an interview with PBS's Jim Lehrer, the president was asked, "You *had* no sexual relationship with this young woman [emphasis added]?" The president replied, "There *is* not a sexual relationship [emphasis added]. That is accurate. We are doing our best to cooperate here, but we don't know much yet. And that's all I can say now."

The change in tense may or may not be significant; Mr. Clinton is well known, and rightly known, for deceiving the public through the use of slippery wording. When asked during the 1992 campaign whether he had ever smoked marijuana, Mr. Clinton answered he had "never broken the laws of my country." He later admitted he smoked marijuana in England. When he was asked by *60 Minutes* correspondent Steve Kroft, "I'm assuming from your answer that you're categorically denying that you ever had an affair with Gennifer Flowers," he answered, "I've said that before, and so has she." Six years later, when he was asked under oath whether he ever had sexual relations with Ms. Flowers, he answered yes. And in an almost eerie anticipation of later circumstances, Mr. Clinton tells Ms. Flowers how to keep the public from finding out about their affair: "I just think that if everybody's on record denying it, you've got no problem."

In any event, according to *The New Yorker* magazine, it was only after Mr. Clinton's Hollywood friend Harry Thomason flew to Washington to help the president that he delivered his indignant, jaw-clenching, finger-waving denial of sexual relations with "that woman, Miss Lewinsky." Bill Clinton delivered his lines like an old Hollywood pro. He was almost believable.

But the president's denial isn't enough insurance. The Clinton administration recognizes the denial may not hold up, and incontrovertible evidence of lying under oath may emerge. So Lanny Davis and others are laying the groundwork for another Clinton defense, which goes something like this: even if the president of the United States lied under oath, it is irrelevant. Why? Because the lies the president may have told during his deposition in the Paula Jones case don't matter. Why? Because the testimony was about a sexual matter in a civil case that was ultimately dismissed—and the testimony itself was not "material." That is, even if Mr. Clinton did lie about the Lewinsky matter during his deposition in the Jones case, the president's testimony was unlikely to influence the course of the case.

The legal writer Stuart Taylor has made several points in response. First, "the prevailing view at the Clinton Justice Department is that a sworn lie in a civil lawsuit can lead to a perjury conviction even if the lawsuit ends up being dismissed." Second, the legal threshold for materiality is, in the words of Attorney General Reno, "extremely low." And third, the Starr investigation centers on a broad conspiracy to obstruct justice—and under obstruction statutes, materiality need not be proven. (Mr. Taylor, by the way, is a registered Democrat who voted for Mr. Clinton in 1992.) In addition: as a matter of law, it is *irrelevant* if the case was subsequently dismissed; materiality is measured at the time the false statement was made, without regard to subsequent events.

There is also (for Mr. Clinton) this inconvenient fact: the Clinton Justice Department has argued that lying under oath, about oral sex, in a civil case, can lead to a perjury conviction. David Tell, the editorial writer for *The Weekly Standard,* points out that in

United States v. Battalino, the Department of Justice prosecuted a Veterans Administration staff psychiatrist who had falsely testified under oath that she did not have a sexual encounter during a June 27, 1991, office visit with one Ed Arthur. Arthur had filed a civil tort claim against Dr. Battalino and the VA, alleging he had been the victim of medical malpractice. It turns out that Mr. Arthur had recorded telephone conversations in which Dr. Battalino admitted to the June 27 rendezvous. Attorney General Reno, charging that Dr. Battalino "did corruptly endeavor to influence, obstruct and impede the due administration of justice in connection with a pending proceeding before a court of the United States," concluded that the doctor's denial under oath "was false and misleading in that the defendant in fact had performed oral sex on Arthur in her Boise, Idaho VA office on June 27, 1991." Within four days of being charged, Battalino pleaded guilty to one count of obstruction of justice. At the behest of the Clinton administration, Battalino was sentenced to one year of probation, including six months of home detention with electronic monitoring, and fined $3,600—this, Tell writes, "'simply' for deception about oral sex in a civil case. Why should exactly the same standard of justice, for exactly the same offense, not clearly apply to Bill Clinton himself?"

Keep in mind, too, that if Mr. Clinton lied under oath—which this particular defense assumes—the president did not know at the time of his lie that the case would be dismissed. Mr. Clinton only knew that he had sworn under oath to tell the truth; the fact that the case was eventually dismissed, or that the lie may not have been "material," does not change the moral reality.

Finally, suppose for the sake of the argument that Mr. Clinton's lie under oath was not, in fact, "material." Is the new presidential standard that it's fine to lie under oath so long as the lie occurs in a civil case and the charges are dismissed on the grounds that they are immaterial? Call this defining honesty down. Or call it one more Clinton Defense.

II

We now move to the Carville Defense. James Carville and others have advised the president to assert his Fifth Amendment right against self-incrimination.

The president is trying to have it both ways; he publicly insists he is cooperating with the investigation even as he does everything in his power to impede it. In January, he promised the American people famously he would get to the bottom of the scandal and its specific allegations:

"Now there are a lot of other questions that are, I think, very legitimate. You have a right to ask them. You and the American people have a right to get answers. We are working very hard to comply, get all the requests for information up here. And we will give you as many answers as we can, as soon as we can, at the appropriate time, consistent with our obligation to also cooperate with the investigations. And that's not a dodge; that's really what I've—what I've—I've talked [about] with our people. I want to do that. I'd like for you to have more rather than less, sooner rather than later. So we will work through it as quickly as we can and get all those questions out there to you."

The president's promise was a clever lie; it bought him time. Of course, Clinton defenders have a different explanation. The president, they say, was planning to be forthcoming, but circumstances changed; it suddenly turned out that Mr. Starr was "hell-bent on destroying" Mr. Clinton, so it would be "foolhardy" to cooperate.

The problem with this is that Mr. Starr has been the independent counsel since 1994; Mr. Clinton obviously knew what he was dealing with in Judge Starr when, earlier this year, he pledged full cooperation with the independent counsel and "more rather than less, sooner rather than later." Mr. Starr did not change; Mr. Clinton's range of options did. When stonewalling became a viable political strategy, the president fully embraced it, as would many people who had reason to fear a truthful account.

Apologists for the president insist that cooperating with Judge Starr—that is, testifying before a grand jury to respond to allegations that the president committed perjury, suborned perjury, and obstructed justice—means giving the independent counsel all the weapons he needs to railroad an innocent man. Presumably Judge Starr would do this awful deed by convincing the Congress, the public, and a watching world that an innocent president is guilty; after all, there is very little possibility of indicting a sitting president (more about that later).

The "We Can't Possibly Cooperate with Ken Starr" defense rests on the assumption that Judge Starr is extremely corrupt, extremely bold (by attempting the worst political smear in American history), and extremely clever. For it would require of Mr. Starr that he take the president's testimony; willfully twist it beyond recognition; see to it that the president's proclamation of innocence be both unverifiable and unpersuasive; and, finally, convince a majority in the House, and two thirds in the Senate, that for the first time in history a sitting president (in this case, an innocent sitting president) should be impeached and convicted because of high crimes and misdemeanors.

This scenario is as fantastic as Hillary Clinton's assertion that a "vast right-wing conspiracy" is responsible for all her husband's troubles. President Clinton is the most powerful man in the world, and has some of the best lawyers on the planet defending him. The public is more than fair-minded when it comes to judging the president. And congressional impeachment would require a substantial number of Democratic votes. As Professor Jonathan Turley of George Washington University Law School has written, "if Clinton answers the questions truthfully there is little Starr could do to punish an innocent man." (Professor Turley, incidentally, voted for Clinton in 1992.)

Because the president will not tell the truth, he is doing what he can to hide it. This means following, as if it were Holy Writ, Mr. Carville's counsel (and the counsel of his lawyers) to effectively invoke the Fifth Amendment. During his first solo press conference of the year, Mr. Clinton was asked repeatedly about his relationship with Monica Lewinsky and various aspects of the investigation. Here is what he said:

"I have answered it repeatedly and have nothing to add to my former answer."

"I really believe it's important for me not to say any more about this."

"On the claims of executive privilege, I cannot comment on those matters because they are under seal."

"I just don't have anything else to say about that."

"I just have nothing to say."

When asked by ABC's Sam Donaldson if, as a general standard for presidents, "does it matter if you have committed perjury or in any other sense broken the law," Mr. Clinton was unwilling even to answer that question directly. Here is what he said: "Well, since I have answered the underlying questions, I really believe it's important for me not to say any more about this. I think that I'm, in some ways, the last person who needs to be having a national conversation about this." Perhaps the president is right. Perhaps Bill Clinton is the last person who should speak out about ethical standards for presidents.

So long as it was legally and politically possible, the president stuck with his de facto Fifth Amendment defense. Can we therefore make reasonable inferences of wrongdoing? The president's defenders argue no. In response, set aside the fact that in civil cases it is reasonably assumed that a person who invokes the Fifth

Amendment is doing so because his testimony would be self-incriminating; he invokes his right to remain silent in the reasonable belief that telling the truth will hurt him. Set aside the president's acidlike corrosion of the requirement for accountability and procedural regularity in the executive. And set aside the fact that the president is credibly accused of multiple felony crimes; declined multiple requests to testify about those allegations; declined multiple requests to explain his behavior in connection with those allegations to the American people; and allowed his Justice and Treasury Departments to mount multiple specious legal arguments designed to help him maintain that silence.

Apply instead the standards of common sense and everyday life. When for more than a half-year the president—*the nation's chief legal officer*—repeatedly refused to answer, and repeatedly encouraged others to refuse to answer, serious, credible criminal allegations made against him, we are entitled to make reasonable judgments about wrongdoing.

This applies even more so in the case of Bill Clinton. Let's stipulate the obvious: he is among the most voluble and persuasive men to ever sit in the Oval Office. More than that, he is a town hall, feel-your-pain, let's-talk-about-what's-on-your-mind kind of president. He seemingly wants to be a part of *every* conversation going on in America. Here we have a controversy which dominates American conversations. The president is the central player in the controversy; he knows all the relevant facts; he has an unrivaled bully pulpit from which he can speak; and yet he went mute. Faced with the gravest threat to his presidency, from late January through mid-August the president became demure, taciturn, *speechless*. Think for a moment about the revealing irony and incongruity: William Jefferson Clinton as the Great American Sphinx. It appears that only a subpoena helped the president find his voice.

If telling the truth would exonerate President Clinton, its benefits to him would be immediate and exhilarating. He would remove
from his name the stench of scandal; pursue his second-term
agenda free of distraction; and embarrass mightily his critics in
the media and in the opposition party. All this and more is there to
be had—with only one caveat: the truth must be on the president's
side in order to clear his name and vindicate his character. But it
is not, and so he cannot. We have a president who said he was
"absolutely" prepared to leave unrefuted serious and credible
allegations of wrongdoing. This was without precedent, something
even the founders did not anticipate. All in all, it is both revealing
and damning.

III

Even if overwhelming circumstantial evidence points toward a
sordid sexual affair with Monica Lewinsky and a subsequent criminal cover-up, Clinton apologists aver, we still ought not jump to
hasty conclusions. After all, the president is "innocent until
proved guilty"—and his innocence or guilt, in turn, can only be
determined by the courts, which is where this decision rightly
belongs.

We have seen this defense before. In September 1973, Senator
Bob Dole, then chairman of the Republican party and an ardent
Nixon defender, introduced an unsuccessful Senate resolution to
stop live TV coverage of the congressional Watergate hearings. "It
is time to turn off the TV lights," Mr. Dole said. "It is time to move
the Watergate investigation from the living rooms of America and
put it where it belongs—behind the closed doors of the committee
room and before the judge and jury in the courtroom."

It is a flawed premise to assume the only way to judge that
someone has engaged in wrongdoing, even criminal wrongdoing, is

for the allegations to be proved in a court of law. Bear in mind that Richard Nixon was never found guilty of a crime. He was never indicted. Nor was he impeached. Still, we know he was at the epicenter of a criminal conspiracy.

Nor is it clear that the "let the courts decide" argument even applies in the case of the president. Many, if not most, legal scholars believe it is unconstitutional to indict—and hence possibly subject to criminal punishment—a sitting president. That does not place a president above the law; it merely means that an indictment, if it does come, can come only *after* impeachment and conviction. The framers and ratifiers of the Constitution argued that impeachable offenses must include noncriminal and nonindictable offenses. An impeachment, therefore, is a *political* and not a legal proceeding. It is an instrument that should only be used as a last resort, with extreme caution, in exceptional circumstances, with full recognition of the trauma it can cause. Nevertheless, it is there to protect the public interest against gravely irresponsible, but noncriminal, acts.

In *Federalist Paper No. 65*, Alexander Hamilton wrote: "A well-constituted court for the trial of impeachment is an object not more to be desired than difficult to be obtained in a government wholly elective. The subjects of its jurisdiction are those offenses which proceed from the misconduct of public men . . . from the abuse or violation of some public trust . . . which may with peculiar propriety be denominated POLITICAL."

James Madison believed impeachment should be used for "negligence or perfidy of the chief magistrate." Impeachment was a guarantor of "supplemental security for the good behavior of the public officers." George Mason, a Virginia delegate to the constitutional convention, believed impeachment should be used for "corruption," and South Carolina's Charles Pinckney for those "who behave amiss or betray their public trust."

Joseph Story, a nineteenth-century Supreme Court justice and one of America's most important legal scholars, wrote that impeachment should be used for "what are aptly termed political offenses, growing out of personal misconduct, or gross neglect, or usurpation, or habitual disregard of the public interest."

There are other, more recent, sources whom we can turn to. In 1974 a bright young Yale Law School graduate worked for the House Judiciary committee's impeachment inquiry staff. A February 20 memorandum prepared by the committee's staff offered a comprehensive study of the historic origins of the impeachment process and the issue of criminality. Among its findings:

"To confine impeachable conduct to indictable offenses may well be to set a standard so restrictive as not to reach conduct that might adversely affect the system of government. Some of the most grievous offenses against our constitutional form of government may not entail violations of the criminal law. . . . To limit impeachable conduct to criminal offenses would be incompatible with the evidence . . . and would frustrate the purpose that the framers intended. . . . Impeachment was evolved . . . to cope with both the inadequacy of criminal standards and the impotence of the courts to deal with the conduct of great public figures. It would be anomalous if the framers, having barred criminal sanctions from the impeachment remedy . . . intended to restrict the grounds for impeachment to conduct that was criminal."

By all accounts, twenty-six-year-old staff attorney Hillary Rodham was proud of the report she helped to prepare.

A quarter-century ago Hillary Rodham understood, far better than she does today, the corrupting effect of reducing large civic questions to narrow legal ones. Interpreting the actions of a president solely through a legal prism habituates Americans to think like lawyers instead of citizens. It predisposes people to believe courts are the only arbiters in judging right and wrong. And it fosters an unreasonable and unhealthy reliance on legal structures.

Lest I be misunderstood, let me reiterate that respect for law, and for the rule of law, is a matter of paramount importance in a democracy. It should be abundantly clear by now that in my view, President Clinton's flouting of the rule of law has had a devastating effect on our nation and on our view of the presidency. But legalism and the rule of law are two different things. In the hands of skilled and deceitful men, the former can too easily be manipulated to dodge or even subvert the latter, and thus further poison the wells of public life.

On this issue, there are still others from whom we can learn. In his extraordinary 1978 Harvard University commencement address Aleksandr Solzhenitsyn warned Americans of the stupefying effects of a legalistic culture:

"I have spent all my life under a Communist regime and I will tell you that a society without any objective legal scale is a terrible one indeed. But a society with no other scale but the legal one is also less than worthy of man. A society based on the letter of the law and never reaching any higher fails to take advantage of the full range of human possibilities. The letter of the law is too cold and formal to have a beneficial influence on society. Whenever the tissue of life is woven of legalistic relationships, this creates an atmosphere of spiritual mediocrity that paralyzes man's noblest impulses."

In the end, the president's apologists are attempting to redefine the standard of acceptable behavior for a president. Instead of upholding a high view of the office and the men who occupy it, they radically lower our expectation. Anything above a common criminal will do—and even criminal conduct, in some circumstances, is excusable.

Jeremy Rabkin, professor of government at Cornell University, puts it this way: "The standard of acceptable behavior for the president has sunk to what can be proved in a court of law where jurors must find guilt 'beyond a reasonable doubt.' Of course, the minimally acceptable conduct for the chief executive is a disputable political judgment. But as Congress hangs back and allows the 'independent counsel' to proceed with his criminal investigations, we have effectively defined eligibility for continuance in office by the O. J. Simpson standard—anything that can't be proven for absolute certain to a skeptical jury. That is the ultimate constitutional perversion."

That it is. And that, alas, is where we are.

Chapter 6

Judgment

Defense of President Clinton: *Even if President Clinton had an adulterous relationship with Monica Lewinsky and lied under oath about it, defenders of the president argue that we should be tolerant, more forgiving of human frailty, and less judgmental. In support of this view, Clinton defenders often invoke two passages from the Bible. The first is in the eighth chapter of the Gospel of John. Admonishing those who want to stone a woman caught in adultery, Jesus declares, "He who is without sin, cast the first stone." The second passage is from the seventh chapter of the Gospel of Matthew. During His Sermon on the Mount, Christ says, "Judge not, lest you be judged."*

I encountered this biblically based defense when giving a speech to an organization of religious broadcasters earlier this year, in the course of which I criticized the president's unwillingness to explain what happened in the Lewinsky matter. A member of the audience took me to task for "casting stones."

112 | William J. Bennett

During a March 5 interview on the Today *show, the Reverend Billy Graham was asked if he would forgive President Clinton for his alleged affair with Monica Lewinsky. Reverend Graham responded, "I forgive him. I don't know what the average person— but, I mean, certainly I forgive him. Because I know the frailty of human nature and I know how hard it is—especially a strong, vigorous young man like he is. And he has such a tremendous personality that I think the ladies just go wild over him."*

During an April 15 interview with Jerry Falwell, Pat Robertson, and Oral Roberts, CNN's Larry King picked up on Graham's comments. "Billy Graham said on this program he not only prays for [Bill Clinton], loves him, forgives him, understands lust, and is not the one to make a judgment about him. . . . [Graham] totally forgives him. Do you forgive him anything wrong? Why criticize him?" Later in the interview Mr. King pressed Pat Robertson hard, saying, "You're judging, of course, you're judging." In other words, if even Billy Graham (no radical liberal, he) has forgiven the president, why can't the president's critics? And to Christians in particular, the message is this: you cannot both forgive a president and judge him.

Martin Walker, European editor of Britain's Guardian, *is hopeful that tolerance will prevail over what he perceives as puritanical judgmentalism. "People, however furiously their Puritan passions may flame, cannot indefinitely withstand the temptations of the flesh. They grow tired of the moral rigors of a Savonarola [fifteenth-century Italian Dominican religious reformer]. They become ashamed of the excesses of a Torquemada [fifteenth-century Spanish Dominican monk who promulgated, and ruthlessly enforced, rules for the Inquisition]. They understand that Christianity has survived, not because it has such implacably austere defenders, but because it was inspired by one who embraced an adulteress and said, 'Let him who is without sin among you cast the first stone.'"*

Former Senator George McGovern, after professing in the Los Angeles Times *that his Methodist faith does not permit him to countenance illicit sex, reminds his fellow "Christian communicants" about the warning, "Let him who is without sin cast the first stone." In speaking of the investigation of Kenneth Starr, Senator McGovern invokes the image of the Salem witch trials, and goes on to ask for "a little more compassion and a little less persecution."*

The Reverend J. Philip Wogaman, a Christian ethicist and pastor of the church Bill and Hillary Clinton attend, was interviewed by the New York Times *about the president's alleged sexual misconduct. Wogaman told the* Times *he is a preacher who likes to weigh the relativity of issues. The only absolute is God, according to Wogaman, and when human beings make absolutes out of a "cultural expression" like heterosexuality or sexual fidelity, then they have succumbed to "idolatry."*

Among the factors keeping the president's public approval rating so high despite wave after wave of scandal is a firm public embrace of nonjudgmentalism. One Republican voter interviewed by the Washington Post *said, "[Clinton] is no different than anybody else. So why should I judge?"*

Eppie Lederer (aka Ann Landers) told Frank Rich, a New York Times *columnist, that in the wake of the accusations and revelations against President Clinton, she was (pleasantly) surprised at the lack of outrage among her readers. "There was so little negative mail and such an outpouring of support [she receives two thousand letters a day]. I have concluded this is a very popular President. They're saying it's not our business, and we don't care. . . . This is not just sophisticated New York and California. This is Middle America." When asked if the public's refusal to condemn Mr. Clinton signals some kind of moral collapse, she replied she thought just the opposite. According to Ms. Landers, "People are much more willing to forgive now. They are more permissive. They are more realistic. This is the way life is. Not all husbands are faithful. . . . I've been doing this 43 years. The country has been going in this direction for some time. I don't think it's just the Clintons. We're getting to be more forgiving as a people. It's a good thing."*

Response

The core of this defense is: we are wrong to judge the president because the Bible itself says we ought not to judge or "cast stones"; even if one is not persuaded by the biblical injunctions, the harsh judgmentalism displayed by the president's critics is contrary to an open-minded, pluralistic society like ours; and the extent to which the public is not outraged by the president's conduct (even if you assume he had an affair and broke laws to cover it up) is a healthy sign of tolerance, forgiveness, and cultural sophistication. I disagree with all three assertions.

I

Many defenders of President Clinton are attempting to use theological arguments to shield the president from criticism. It is important, therefore, to examine briefly the merits of these arguments by the very biblical standard they invoke, in order to determine whether they are making a correct scriptural application—or whether, in fact, they are bending Scripture to justify preordained (and politically expedient) conclusions. Let us therefore take a closer look.

But Jesus went to the Mount of Olives. At dawn He appeared again in the temple courts, where all the people gathered around Him, and He sat down to teach them. The teachers of the law and the Pharisees brought in a woman caught in adultery. They made her stand before the group and said to Jesus, "Teacher, this woman was caught in the act of adultery. In the Law Moses commanded us to stone such women. Now what do you say?" They were using this question as a trap, in order to have a basis for accusing Him. But Jesus bent down and started to write on the ground with His finger. When they kept on questioning Him, He straightened up and said to them, "If any one of you is without sin, let him be the first to throw a stone at her." Again He stooped down and wrote on the ground. At this, those who heard began to go away one at a time, the older ones first, until only Jesus was left, with the woman still standing there. Jesus straightened up and asked her, "Woman, where are they? Has no one condemned you?" "No one, sir," she said. "Then neither do I condemn you," Jesus declared. "Go now and leave your life of sin." (John 8:1–11)

There is much to learn from this passage: the need for a generous and compassionate spirit toward others; the need for a thoughtful examination of our own failures; the need to resist the impulse quickly and easily to condemn those who have fallen; the willingness to give someone a second chance.

But what the Clinton defenders almost always leave out is the end of the exchange, when Jesus tells the adulterous woman, "go now and leave your life of sin." (The woman, it is worth pointing out, did not deny the charge, stonewall, or lie to cover it up.) Jesus was *not* providing a pardon, to be granted easily, cheaply, without cost or repentance. And the point was surely not that wrongdoing should be tolerated or that sin is inconsequential; in Christian doctrine, indeed, sin is so consequential that only Christ's sacrificial death on a cross could remit it. Jesus appears to have been asking the woman to learn from her mistake and change her ways—and He was confident she would.

> *Do not judge, or you too will be judged. For in the same way you judge others, you will be judged, and with the measure you use, it will be measured to you. Why do you look at the speck of sawdust in your brother's eye and pay not attention to the plank in your own eye?*
>
> *How can you say to your brother, "Let me take the speck out of your eye," when all the time there is a plank in your own eye? You hypocrite, first take the plank out of your own eye, and then you will see clearly to remove the speck from your brother's eye. Do not give dogs what is sacred; do not throw your pearls to pigs. If you do, they may trample them under their feet, and then turn and tear you to pieces." (Matthew 7:1–6)*

Matthew's "judge not" passage is a warning to Christians not to judge self-righteously, uncharitably, hypocritically, hypercritically, in a spirit of harsh condemnation. It is a valuable reminder of how easy it is to fall into traps set by a heart grown cold and hard. It is a reminder, too, that all of us need to be appropriately self-critical. But this passage is not—it *cannot* be—a call to withhold all judgment or never to express a critical opinion of another.

Note that at the end of the passage in Matthew, Christ instructs us not to "give dogs what is sacred" and not to "throw your pearls to pigs." But of course this means that one has to make discriminating judgments about others. The implied conclusion by Clinton apologists that Christ-like forgiveness should render a person incapable of moral criticism collapses under the sheer weight of biblical evidence. Throughout the New Testament, Christians are called upon to judge false teaching; bad doctrine; idolatry; immorality; and more.

For Christians, the crucifixion is history's supreme act of sacrificial love. Still, this same Jesus, in the twenty-third chapter of the Gospel of Matthew, unambiguously judges and exposes those who He feared were leading his followers to disaster as "blind fools," a "brood of vipers," full of "hypocrisy and wickedness." Elsewhere in Matthew, Jesus criticizes a "wicked and adulterous generation." The Gospels tell us that as Jesus entered the temple area in Jerusalem, He drove out those who were buying and selling, and overturned the tables of the money changers who had turned a "house of prayer" into a "den of robbers."

The Book of James urges us to get rid of "all moral filth and the evil that is so prevalent." Saint Peter wrote that we ought not conform to the "evil desires you had when you lived in ignorance." Saint Paul, who wrote the beautiful exposition on love in I Corinthians 13, chastises the very same church in Corinth because complacently it has accepted immorality in its midst. He even urges members to expel a man who is an adulterer. Saint Paul was aggrieved that the church took so lax a view of so serious a matter; he knew that collapsing moral standards in the church would corrupt it. The Book of Romans tells us that government was established to restrain evil and punish wrongdoing. It speaks of God's "righteous judgment" and warns us not to show contempt for the riches of God's kindness, tolerance, and patience.

Neither Christ, Saint Paul, the Apostle Peter, nor James was harsh or intolerant, unforgiving or arbitrary. They deeply loved humanity, and their own followers. They wanted to protect them, and the young church, from harm. But throughout the entire Bible—in the Old and New Testaments, in book after book, in passage after passage—righteousness is exalted and sin and wickedness are denounced.

The attempt to use God's forgiveness as a pretext to excuse moral wrong is a dangerous (and old) heresy known as antinomianism—

literally "against the law." Essentially it rejects the moral law as a relevant part of Christian experience. The thought that God's grace, given to us through Christ's death at Golgotha, would justify licentiousness has long been considered contemptible by saints and scholars throughout the ages. And rightly so.

II

Billy Graham is among the monumental religious figures of recent times. I have great personal regard for him, his ministry, and the way he has led a life free from scandal. But his comments about forgiving the president are disconcerting. And wrong.

Graham comes dangerously close to justifying the president's infidelity when he speaks of Bill Clinton as a "strong, vigorous young man" with a "tremendous personality"—for whom "the ladies just go wild."* But of course, the concern about Bill Clinton is not that the ladies go wild for him, but that he goes wild for them. That after all is the basis of the sworn testimony of Kathleen Willey, Paula Jones, and several state troopers who testified that then–Governor Bill Clinton used them to procure women for him.

And what is it precisely that Billy Graham forgives the president for? What has the president admitted doing? Billy Graham forgives him for something the president has denied in his deposition ever having done.

What we have, then, is forgiveness being granted without admission of guilt, without apology, without repentance. Forgiveness is becoming a synonym for lax standards and tolerance for (and acceptance of) transgressions. And that is a terrible thing to allow to happen. For in Christian doctrine, forgiveness comes at an extraordinarily high cost. One of the twentieth century's important

---

*To the Reverend Graham's credit, shortly after his remarks he wrote an op-ed about the importance of moral character in political leaders.

theologians, Dietrich Bonhoeffer, wrote about what he called "cheap grace."

According to Bonhoeffer: "Cheap grace means grace sold on the market like cheapjacks' wares. The sacraments, the forgiveness of sin, and the consolations of religion are thrown away at cut prices. . . . [Cheap grace] amounts to the justification of sin without the justification of the repentant sinner who departs from sin and from whom sin departs. Cheap grace is not the kind of forgiveness which frees us from the toils of sin. Cheap grace is the grace we bestow on ourselves."

We violate God's canons of justice when we invoke forgiveness casually, trivially, promiscuously. And even in those moments when forgiveness is given properly—and such moments of "costly grace" can be an extraordinary witness to the world—the person forgiven should *still* be held accountable for his acts. We reap what we sow—even when there is contrition. Remember: God forgave David for his infidelity with Bathsheba and for the death of her husband, Uriah, but terrible tragedy still visited David's life—including the death of his infant son. In 1984 Pope John Paul II walked into a prison cell in Rome and took the hand of Mehmet Ali Agca, the man who shot him in an assassination attempt, and forgave him. It is worth noting that Agca admitted to his crime and said, "I am repentant for the attack on the pope." The pope was the individual who had been wronged; it seems to me that this admirable act was a human type of divine forgiveness. But nobody, not even the pope, believed that Mehmet Ali Agca should walk out of the prison and into freedom.

III

So much for a (brief) discussion of the theological justification for nonjudgmentalism. But there are many Clinton supporters who arrive at the same conclusion through secular instead of religious reasoning. The gravamen of their argument is that "judgmentalism"—particularly moral judgmentalism—is out of place in a pluralistic society like ours. This appeal is a shrewd one; since the Lewinsky story broke, one deep, persistent attitude running through large segments of the public is an admixture of nonjudgmentalism and indifference. It often takes the form of the (rhetorical) question: who are *we* to judge?

Here is what a *New York Times* poll found: "Even if it turns out that Mr. Clinton obstructed justice by lying under oath or urging Ms. Lewinsky to lie, most Americans think that matter should be dropped or that he should simply admit it and apologize. Only 21 percent favor his resignation in that situation, while 12 percent say that Congress should begin impeachment proceedings." In other words, only a third of all Americans favor the resignation of the president, or impeachment proceedings, even if the president obstructed justice.

These are examples of what sociologist Alan Wolfe refers to as America's new Eleventh Commandment: "Thou shalt not judge." In his recent book, *One Nation After All,* Wolfe closely examines the moral beliefs of eight suburban communities. "Middle-class Americans are reluctant to pass judgment on how other people act and think," writes Wolfe (who I should point out is mostly sanguine about the American moral attitudes he has found). Firm moral convictions have been eroded by tentativeness, uncertainty, diffidence. This new middle-class consensus is not surprising, since during the last thirty years we have witnessed a relentless assault on traditional norms and a profound shift in public attitudes. The tectonic plates have moved.

Why have we been drawn toward a culture of permissiveness? My former philosophy professor John Silber was correct when he spoke of an "invitation to mutual corruption." We are hesitant to impose upon ourselves a common moral code because we want our own exemptions.

This modern allergy to judgments and standards, of which attitudes toward the Clinton scandals are but a manifestation, is deeply problematic, for a defining mark of a good republic is precisely the willingness of its citizens to make judgments about things that matter. In America we do not defer to kings, cardinals, or aristocrats; we rely instead on the people's capacity to make reasonable judgments based on moral principles.

Those who constantly invoke the sentiment of "who are we to judge?" should consider the anarchy that would ensue if we adhered to this sentiment in, say, our courtrooms. Should judges judge? What would happen if those sitting on a jury decided to be "nonjudgmental" about rapists and sexual harassers, embezzlers and tax cheats? Without being "judgmental," Americans would never have put an end to slavery, outlawed child labor, emancipated women, or ushered in the civil rights movement. Nor would we have prevailed against Nazism and Soviet communism, or known how to explain our opposition.

How do we judge a wrong—any wrong whatsoever—when we have gutted the principle of judgment itself? What arguments can be made after we have strip-mined all the arguments of their force, their power, their ability to inspire public outrage? We all know that there are times when we will have to judge others, when it is both right and *necessary* to judge others. If we do not confront the soft relativism that is now disguised as a virtue, we will find ourselves morally and intellectually disarmed.

IV

Clinton defenders like Ann Landers celebrate America's growing "tolerance." What are we to make of this new tolerance which, according to Alan Wolfe, has become a bedrock moral principle of the American middle class?

Tolerance rightly understood serves an important public purpose. In the classical liberal understanding, it means according respect to the beliefs and practices of others, and learning to live peacefully and civilly with one another despite deep differences. Tolerance allows for the "free trade in ideas" (in Justice Oliver Wendell Holmes's phrase), which is the best way to ensure that the right beliefs will emerge. It assumes that all reasoned opinions will get a fair hearing, even when what is said may not be popular. Tolerance can serve as an antidote to the destructive passions inflamed by (among other things) misguided religious beliefs.

So tolerance is a great social good, which is precisely why it needs to be rescued from the reckless attempt to redefine it. For it is a social good only up to a point, and only when its meaning is not massively disfigured. But "tolerance" can be a genuinely harmful force when it becomes a euphemism for moral exhaustion and a rigid or indifferent neutrality in response to every great moral issue—when, in G. K. Chesterton's phrase, it becomes the virtue of people who do not believe in anything. For that paves the road to injustice.

To decry the lack of tolerance in late-twentieth-century America is (as C. S. Lewis once put it) akin to reaching for a fire hose during a flood. A rigid and inflexible embrace of moral truths is not the virus that has invaded America's body politic, nor are we suffering from an oversupply of consistent moral judgments. To the contrary, we live in an era when it has become unfashionable to make judgments on a whole range of very consequential behaviors and attitudes. To take just one example: 70 percent of people between the ages of eighteen and thirty-four say that people who generate a baby out of wedlock should not be subject to moral reproach of any sort.

In the view of many people today, it is imperious to be judgmental. But judgment is not bigotry; and tolerance may just be another term for indifference. If to make judgments of better and worse, good and bad, fit and unfit, sound and unsound, competent and incompetent is to be judgmental, then there is a *need* to be judgmental and no need to apologize for it. For a free people, the ordeal of judgment cannot be shirked. To try to shirk it is not to be sensitive or tolerant, it is to avoid responsibility. Teachers judge the work of their students, and students the work of their teachers. Parents judge their children's study habits and viewing habits, their friends, teachers, and baby-sitters, their manners and appearance, their deportment and language. People judge political candidates and stands on public policy issues. People judge fallibly, with uncertainty, on the basis of the facts; but if they will not judge, they can be rightly suspected of being without convictions. And people without convictions cannot be counted on. And a democracy, more than any other form of government, needs a people on whom you can count.

There is a vital link between reasonable judgment and authentic compassion. Without judgment, there can be no common ethic. No standards. No established authority. No rules to govern behavior. No wise counsel on how best to live. What is at stake here is not an abstract intellectual argument; we see every day the human cost of an increasingly relativistic world, defended by the invocation of "tolerance" and "openness." We see it on angry urban streets. In drug rehabilitation centers. In hospital emergency room admissions. In classrooms that resemble war zones. In crisis pregnancy centers. In foster homes. In divorce courts. And in much more. Moral judgments—thoughtful and careful, but explicit and unapologetic—need to be made, not for the sake of satisfying a "Puritan passion" or a "rigid moralism," but because we human beings live better, more noble, more complete and satisfying lives when we hold ourselves to some common moral understanding.

V

The problem with the advocates of nonjudgmentalism is that real life intrudes, and their nonjudgmentalism goes out the window. Their own rhetoric aside, when pressed, Clinton apologists will confess they are not against judgmentalism in *all* areas. There are, well, some things that society *should* be judgmental about. Tobacco, say. Or environmental polluters. Or the National Rifle Association. Or opponents of racial quotas. Or Ken Starr.

It turns out that while there are very few hard-core nihilists among us, there are plenty of soft-core relativists. What is instructive are the categories where selective judgment applies. What we see is not the kind of commonsense distinctions we make in everyday life but the granting of important moral exemptions because of ideological predilections. The soft-core relativists believe in withholding judgment not abstractly and across the board but in certain a priori categories, starting with the sexual or moral conduct of those political leaders who happen to advance their agenda.

Take the Reverend Wogaman, who believes sexual fidelity is but a nonbinding "cultural expression" and that those of us who consider it a moral absolute have succumbed to "idolatry." His casual dismissal of sexual fidelity as merely a "cultural expression" is hubris of a high order; he is dismissing the accumulated wisdom of the centuries and the clear teaching of his professed faith. He is also making the widespread (postmodern) philosophical error of assuming that morality is merely a product of culture, and that there is no such thing as objective truth. As for moral absolutes turning into "idolatry": Christ taught that the mark of a true believer was to "keep My commandments," of which sexual fidelity is one.

But Wogaman is also being selective. In the nineteenth century, if a legislator were to have argued that the anti-slavery movement was merely a "cultural expression," and termed any effort to resist resegregation "idolatrous," would the Reverend Wogaman have been quite so flexible? He would not. Nor should have been. But here, it turns out that the president's pastor embraces the president's own (liberal) moral absolutes, and in more areas than one. In criticizing the GOP's Contract with America, Wogaman declared "it would be reprehensible for American society to abandon the poor." He referred to the "excesses and brutalities and idolatries of the free market." He told the *Washington Post* that a ban on late-term abortions would be "unfeeling." And he is against those who resist the normalization of the homosexual lifestyle. Strong judgments, all—evidence, even, of judgmentalism.

In his *Los Angeles Times* article, similarly, Senator McGovern issues a stern warning to those who take charges of illicit sex, lying, and perjury seriously. He who is without sin, let him cast the first stone, Mr. McGovern reminds his readers. He urges upon us more "compassion" and less "persecution." But Mr. McGovern then walks over to the rock pile and begins throwing large stones in the direction of independent counsel Kenneth Starr and other critics of the president. He even compares them to the executioners of the accused Salem witches. So much for more "compassion" and less "persecution."

Let me conclude this chapter by proposing some "common ground." Let's acknowledge the intellectual emptiness of the Ann Landers position, whereby "tolerance" on sexual matters is always honored and judgmentalism always eschewed. It seems to me that we would do better to heed the words of one Democratic president who, in a candidly judgment-laden statement, proclaimed that "individual character involves honoring and embracing certain core ethical values: honesty, respect, responsibility. . . . Parents must teach their children from the earliest age the difference between right and wrong." And, this president went on to say, "we must all do our part."

In signing this proclamation during National Character Week in 1996, Bill Clinton was right; when it comes to embracing and exemplifying core ethical values, we must all do our part. All of us—including, perhaps even especially, our presidents.

Conclusion

The most important thing was that the rule of law should prevail; the president must comply with the law. This depends whether the people, in a moral and political sense, will rise up and force him to comply with the law. Will they understand what is at stake? Because, ultimately, all their liberties were at stake.
—Archibald Cox, the special prosecutor fired by Richard Nixon almost a quarter-century ago, on Watergate

Sunlight is the best disinfectant, Justice Louis Brandeis once said. The preceding pages are an attempt to cast sunlight on the words and the most popular arguments made on behalf of President Clinton. I have explained why I believe they are wrong and harmful; cannot withstand scrutiny; and are not worthy of a great people.

In reviewing how the debate has progressed since late January 1998, I am struck by the contrived quality of the defenses made on

behalf of Bill Clinton. They are the words of hired guns, spin-
ners, and partisans. They have about them a falseness and artifi-
ciality.

We see these "passionate" defenses mounted by people who
have willingly shielded themselves from the truth. Press spokesman Mike McCurry was asked whether he wanted to know the
truth behind the scandal. He answered in a moment of unguarded
candor, "God, no. No, I really don't want to know." And then he
said this: "Knowing the truth means that you have to tell the
truth." Truth is the one thing the president and his defenders cannot countenance.

But deception often works, at least for a time. And it is a fact
that there is little outrage about the president's misconduct—even
among Americans who assume allegations of sexual and criminal
wrongdoing are true. For example, immediately after he was
rocked by serious and credible allegations of wrongdoing, Mr.
Clinton's approval ratings went up, way up—as high as 79 percent, according to an NBC/*Wall Street Journal* poll. And months
after the story broke, as damning circumstantial evidence continued to accumulate, his approval rating (60-plus percent) settled in
at the highest level of his presidency.

What explains this seeming public indifference toward, and
even acceptance of, the president's scandals? The explanations
most often put forth include very good economic times; scandal
fatigue; the fact that a tawdry sexual relationship makes people
queasy; the president's hyperaggressive, relentless, and effective
spin team; the inclination to withhold judgment until more facts
are known or give the president the benefit of the doubt; the fact
that there are few leaders in any realm (religious, business, and
the academy among them) who have articulated the case against
the president; and the fact that Republican leadership—the Loyal
Opposition—has been quiescent and inconsistent in its comments
about the Clinton scandal, apparently afraid of voter backlash.

These are plausible explanations. And still. I cannot shake the thought that the widespread loss of outrage against this president's misconduct tells us something fundamentally important about our condition. Our commitment to long-standing American ideals has been enervated. We desperately need to recover them, and soon. They are under assault.

Professor Hadley Arkes of Amherst College recalls the old joke about the lawyer who is promised unbounded success in business and love, to be paid for in the end but only at the price of giving up his soul. And he asks: "What's the catch?"

According to Professor Arkes, "The accomplishment of Bill Clinton is that he has made the country into one large lawyer-joke. Clinton has marked off the record of an incorrigible liar, faithless to his wife, who cannot be trusted to honor any law beyond his own interest—and the public says, 'Yes—but what is the problem?'"

The problem is that we are giving license not only to Mr. Clinton's corruption, but possibly to our own as well. In his influential 1978 essay *The Power of the Powerless*, Václav Havel wrote about daily life under communist rule in Eastern Europe. The Czech regime was thoroughly permeated with hypocrisy and lies. And there were citizens, he wrote, who "live[d] within the lie." What he meant by this phrase was that every greengrocer, every clerk who agreed to display official slogans not reflecting his own beliefs, or who voted in elections known to be farcical, or who feigned agreement at political meetings, normalized falsification. Individuals may not have believed all the falsifications, Havel wrote, but they behaved as though they did, or they at least tolerated them in silence. Each individual who lived the lie, who capitulated to "ideological pseudo-reality," became a petty instrument of the regime. This led to a *de-moralized* person, upon which the system, in turn, depended.

This is what President Clinton and his defenders will do to us if we finally accept, and in accepting, approve, his actions and their arguments. We will become complicit in his lies. We will live within the lies.

In living memory, the chief threats to American democracy have come from without: first, Nazism and Japanese imperialism, and, later, Soviet communism. But these wars, hot and cold, ended in spectacular American victories. The threats we now face are from within. They are far different, more difficult to detect, more insidious: decadence, cynicism, and boredom.

Writing about corruption in democratic government, Alexis de Tocqueville warned about "not so much the immorality of the great as the fact that immorality may lead to greatness." When private citizens impute a ruler's success "mainly to some of his vices . . . an odious connection is thus formed between the ideas of turpitude and power, unworthiness and success, utility and dishonor." The rulers of democratic nations, Tocqueville said, "lend the authority of the government to the base practices of which they are accused. They afford dangerous examples, which discourage the struggles of virtuous independence."

Tocqueville recognized, too, that democratic citizens wouldn't be conscious of this tendency, and in fact would probably disagree that it even existed. This is what makes it all the more dangerous; the corrupt actions of democratic leaders influence the public in subtle ways which often go unnoticed among citizens. This sort of decay is gradual, difficult to perceive over a short period of time, and terribly dangerous.

Which brings us back to Bill Clinton. If there is no consequence to the president's repeated betrayal of public trust and his abuses of power, it will have a profound impact on our political and civic culture. Bill Clinton and his defenders are defining personal morality down; radically lowering the standards of what we expect from our president; and changing for the worse the way politics is and will be practiced. Recall the words of John Dean: "If Watergate had succeeded, what would have been put into the system for years to come? People thinking the way Richard Nixon thought, and thinking that is the way it should be. It would have been a travesty; it would have been frightening."

We find ourselves at this familiar juncture today. It would be a travesty, and frightening, to legitimize Mr. Clinton's ethics and the arguments made on their behalf. But we are getting close, disconcertingly close, to doing just that. "He's strictly one of a kind," *Washington Post* columnist Mary McGrory wrote, "our first president to be strengthened by charges of immorality."

You will often hear Clinton apologists argue that to take a stand against the president's misconduct will send the signal that anyone who is not a saint need not apply for the job. Nonsense. We do not expect our presidents to be men of extraordinary virtue, who have lived lives of near perfection. We should not even expect all our presidents to have the sterling character of, say, a Washington or a Lincoln, although we should hope for it, and certainly honor it, on those rare occasions where we find it.

We have every right, however, to expect individuals who, taken in the totality of their acts, are decent and trustworthy. This is not an impossible standard; there are many examples we can look to— Truman, Eisenhower, Carter, and Reagan, to name just four men who served six terms since World War II. These are men, like all of us, who had an assortment of flaws and failings. They made mistakes. But at the end of the day, they were men whose character, at least, we could count on.

Bill Clinton's is not. The difference between these men and Mr. Clinton is the difference between common human frailty and corruption. That we accept the latter as common is a measure of how low our standards have dropped. We have to aim higher, and expect more, from our presidents and from ourselves.

———

In the introduction I wrote that if the arguments made in defense of Bill Clinton become the coin of the public realm, we will have committed an unthinking act of moral and intellectual disarmament. Here is one specific example of what is now becoming a thoroughly mainstream, perfectly respectable point of view: in order to cover up an adulterous relationship between the president and a young White House intern, acts of perjury and obstruction of justice should be considered inconsequential. That this matter is even the subject of a serious national debate is revealing and alarming. It was the *New York Times* which offered this eloquent reminder of what was once a common, elementary-grade civics lesson:

"Law is the keystone of American society and political culture. If it does not apply to small matters concerning this President, the day will come when the public will be asked to believe that it should be ignored in large matters concerning some other President. Neither Mr. Clinton's political convenience nor Mr. Starr's clumsiness must tempt us into paying so high a price. The rule of law, whether applied to matters trivial or grand, is the central magic of the American governmental experience. To abandon it today will lead to peril tomorrow."

Perhaps the history books will describe the Clinton era as a time during which (to recall the words of John Adams) the president of the United States insidiously betrayed, and wantonly trifled away, public trust. When, rocked with serious, credible allegations of grave misconduct and violations of law, the president retreated for as long as he could to a gilded bunker, obstinately and "absolutely" unwilling to rebut troubling allegations made against him. And the history books may describe how a diffident public, when confronted with all the evidence of wrongdoing and all the squalor, simply shrugged its shoulders. And, finally, that William Jefferson Clinton really was the representative man of our time, when the overwhelming majority of Americans no longer believed that presidential character mattered, and that no man, not even a president, was accountable to the law.

Perhaps this is what it will all come to. But we do not yet know. More acts must be played out in this manifestly sordid, but now manifestly important, national drama. We shall see. As a self-governing nation, it is finally up to us. Not a court of law. Not Ken Starr. Us.

One temptation, the very modern temptation, is not to care, or at least to pretend not to care; to suspend judgment, avert our gaze, minimize what is happening, hope the Clinton scandals will soon pass, having wrought minimal damage. But that is something we ought not allow. It is a flight from reality.

Here is my hope. American citizens know better—and they will demonstrate that indeed they do know better. Americans will realize they are being played for fools by the president and his defenders. They will declare, with confidence, that a lie is a lie, an oath is an oath, corruption is corruption. And truth matters.

Here is the simple basis for my hope: we remain American citizens. This appellation has a hallowed standing in the history of nations, for we are heirs to history's most precious political tradition. To be called an American citizen is perhaps the proudest title to which any citizen, at any time, in any country, could ever claim. It is that great a privilege. It is that high an honor.

As such, it entails certain obligations and responsibilities. Today the ideals of American citizenship are under assault by a corrupt, and corrupting, president. He is America's Duke and Dauphin, treating us as if we were the credulous inhabitants of the small Arkansas town in Mark Twain's great American novel, *The Adventures of Huckleberry Finn*, with Mr. Clinton performing his own fraudulent dramas. Mr. Clinton has tarnished, and will continue to tarnish, the highest office in our land. He deserves our repudiation. And if President Clinton, credibly accused of multiple felony crimes, does not provide to the American people a full, plausible, and exculpatory explanation, he deserves impeachment.

Americans would do well to recall the ancient words of Aristotle. He wrote that those are to be praised who are angry at the proper things and the proper people, who are angry as they ought, when they ought, and as long as they ought.

Even during times of comfort and ease, there is an appropriate moment for anger at the proper things, and with the proper person. In our time, the thing is corruption, the person is the president. These are not pleasant matters. But they are supremely important ones. My hope is that those history books of tomorrow will accord not shame but praise and honor to those American citizens who wanted to see justice prevail and who refused to allow reasonable outrage to die. Who hold within them a noble and ennobling human sentiment: *amor patriae.* Love of country.

Afterword

At the time of this writing, President Clinton has promised to testify before the grand jury. The air is full of speculation as to what he will or will not say. Most Americans would like the president to give a truthful, credible explanation of the sordid facts that have been revealed since January 21, 1998. President Clinton *may* give an explanation that is at least partially true. But Americans know in their hearts, from their experience, that a statement can be partly true and still not candid, forthright, or honorable.

Regardless of what the president says, however, tremendous damage has already been done. Pernicious arguments have been made in his defense. The office of the presidency has been badly tarnished and corrupted. And Bill Clinton is the responsible party. Those facts will not change.

August 5, 1998

Afterword to the New Edition

To his closest advisers, Clinton said, "Thank God for public opinion."

—Bob Woodward, *Shadow: Five Presidents and the Legacy of Watergate*

Much has happened since August 5, 1998, when I finished writing *The Death of Outrage.* Among the notable events:

- After seven months of repeated denials, on August 17 the president admitted an "inappropriate" sexual relationship with Monica Lewinsky, a young former White House intern. The president's admission was made only after he was forced by the threat of subpoena to testify before a federal grand jury and because the Office of the Independent Counsel had established irrefutable evidence of the affair (i.e., Mr. Clinton's DNA matched the semen stain on a dress Ms. Lewinsky had turned over to prosecutors).

· On September 9, independent counsel Kenneth W. Starr submitted a report to the United States Congress which, according to Mr. Starr, contained "substantial and credible information . . . that may constitute grounds for impeachment." Among the independent counsel's findings: in an attempt to cover up his illicit affair with Ms. Lewinsky the president lied under oath to a federal grand jury; lied under oath in a civil deposition; endeavored to obstruct justice; and failed in his constitutional duty to faithfully execute the laws.

· On November 13, the president reached an out-of-court settlement with Paula Corbin Jones, agreeing to pay her $850,000 to drop her sexual harassment lawsuit.

· On December 19, the United States House of Representatives, for only the second time in history, impeached the president of the United States. By a vote of 228–206, the House approved an article of impeachment accusing the president of providing "perjurious, false and misleading testimony to the grand jury." And by a vote of 221–212, the House approved a second article of impeachment accusing the president of obstruction of justice.

· On February 12, 1999, the United States Senate, needing a two-thirds vote, failed to convict the president on either article of impeachment (the final vote was 55–45 on the perjury count and 50–50 on obstruction of justice). A number of Democratic senators who voted to acquit President Clinton believe he *did* commit felony crimes but argued that those acts do not rise to the level of "high crimes and misdemeanors," the constitutional threshold for impeachment, conviction, and removal from office.

• On April 12, U.S. District Judge Susan Webber Wright of Arkansas held President Clinton in contempt of court, saying he had willfully provided false testimony under oath about his relationship with Monica Lewinsky in the sexual misconduct lawsuit filed by Paula Corbin Jones. In her thirty-two-page ruling, Judge Wright said "clear and convincing evidence" shows that Mr. Clinton gave "false, misleading and evasive answers that were designed to obstruct the judicial process" in the Jones sexual harassment lawsuit (Judge Wright specifically cited the president's assertion that he was never alone with Ms. Lewinsky and that he did not have a sexual relationship with the former White House intern). Judge Wright's actions mark the first time in history an American president has been held in contempt of court. The president has chosen not to challenge Judge Wright's ruling.

And now, twenty-one months after the story first broke, it is said from almost all quarters that the Clinton-Lewinsky scandal has reached its denouement; in the words of one well-known columnist, this story is "*so over.*" The argument is that it is in everybody's best interest for the country to "come to closure" and "move on," to which my response is: moving on is not so easy. This matter won't evaporate like morning mist simply because the impeachment trial has concluded. While this scandal no longer dominates newspaper headlines, there continue to be aftershocks. The president's squalid affair and his subsequent criminal acts have done palpable damage to the nation. For the better part of a year Mr. Clinton engaged in a full-scale assault on the presidency, the Constitution, the rule of law, truth, marriage vows, solemn promises, the integrity of words, the reputations of truth-tellers. It is an affectation to say we can simply "move on" in the wake of all of this. We will keep returning to it because many Americans understand, at a deep level, that justice has not been done. Bill Clinton's year of scandal will continue to reverberate, gnaw at our conscience, rattle around in our minds. For we know things, deeply troubling things, that we did not know before.

Many of us knew when he took office that Bill Clinton was a man of questionable character, but few among us could have anticipated how manifestly corrupt he is. The last year and a half was vivid proof that Bill Clinton is willing to commit criminal acts to maintain the thing that matters most to him: his political viability.

When the Lewinsky story first broke, Dick Morris, the president's former political adviser, received a call from Mr. Clinton, who was desperate for advice ("Oh, God," Mr. Clinton told Morris, "this is just awful"). According to Morris's grand jury testimony, he told the president, "There's a great capacity for forgiveness in this country and you should consider tapping into it." The president responded, "But what about the legal thing? You know, the legal thing?" Morris suggested that he take a poll and the president agreed. Morris then called back, telling the president that the American public was willing to forgive the president for adultery, but not for perjury or obstruction of justice. Based on a poll result—a *poll result*—Mr. Clinton decided against telling the truth; instead, the president told Morris, "Well, we just have to win, then."

For Bill Clinton, "to win" meant lying repeatedly, with forethought, in civil litigation, before a federal grand jury, and in response to questions posed by the House Judiciary Committee. It meant obstructing justice on the matters of gifts, job searches, and the filing of a false affidavit, and in his attempts to coach and influence the testimony of his secretary, Betty Currie. "To win" meant to commit deliberate violations of law.

We know other things as well, such as: the president of the United States is a pathological liar. During the Lewinsky scandal he lied to his family, his friends, his lawyers, his aides, his cabinet, his party,

the United States Congress, and, emphatically, to his fellow citizens
("I want you to listen to me. I'm going to say this again. I did not have
sexual relations with that woman, Miss Lewinsky. I never told anybody to lie, not a single time. Never. These allegations are false.").
He then lied about his lies. He encouraged his supporters and aides
to publicly defend, and therefore become complicit in, his lies. In
the words of David Schippers, the majority counsel of the House
Judiciary Committee, "There's no one left to lie to."

Bill Clinton is also an incredible user of women, willing to treat
a "girl" (as he called Ms. Lewinsky in his grand jury testimony) as
a sex toy. In his testimony Mr. Clinton said that, "I regret that what
began as a friendship" with Ms. Lewinsky came to include "inappropriate behavior." But this claim, like so many others, is untrue.
According to Ms. Lewinsky the sexual affair began immediately
after they met. She testified that she wasn't sure the president even
knew her name until after the third sexual encounter, and the two
had "their first lengthy and personal conversation" after their *sixth*
sexual encounter.

But Mr. Clinton does more than use women; when necessary, he
savages them. His preferred instrument is destroying reputations
by spreading falsehoods. Consider what the president told White
House aide Sidney Blumenthal (according to Blumenthal's February 5, 1999, Senate trial testimony):

*Q. Did the President then give you his account of what happened
between him and Monica Lewinsky?*

A. As I recall, he did.

Q. What did the president tell you?

*A. He spoke fairly rapidly, as I recall, at that point and said that she
had come on to him and made a demand for sex, that he had
rebuffed her, turned her down, and that she threatened him. And
he said that she said to him that she was called "the stalker" by
her peers and that she hated the term, and that she would claim*

that they had had an affair whether they had or they hadn't,
and that she would tell people.
Q. *Do you remember him also saying that the reason Monica Lewin-*
sky would tell people that is because then she wouldn't be known
by her peers as "the stalker" anymore?
A. *Yes, that's right.*

Shortly after the president told Mr. Blumenthal this lie, stories began to appear in the media reporting that the White House "began a whispering campaign that Lewinsky was 'unstable'" and that Lewinsky was known as "the stalker." Journalists Christopher Hitchens and his wife, Carol Blue, signed affidavits saying that at a lunch Mr. Blumenthal stated that Monica Lewinsky had been a "stalker," was "crazy," and the president was "the victim" of a predatory and unstable sexually demanding young woman. Had it not been for incontrovertible evidence—the semen-stained dress—Ms. Lewinsky's reputation would have been destroyed by Mr. Clinton and his associates, just as they had destroyed the reputations of Gennifer Flowers, Paula Jones, Kathleen Willey, and others.

Bill Clinton is a man of breathtaking self-indulgence and self-absorption, forever aggrieved, always the victim, more sinned against than sinning, never responsible for the trouble in which he finds himself. In a March 31 interview with CBS's Dan Rather, Mr. Clinton declared that he wasn't troubled at all by the fact that he was impeached; in his words, "I do not regard this impeachment vote as some great badge of shame. I do not." When asked to respond to criticisms that he "parses" words too much (his preferred method of making and defending false and misleading statements), he responded by comparing himself to, presumably, FDR. "You say I parse words," Mr. Clinton said. "That's what they said about President Roosevelt, too. He made a pretty good president." And he cast himself as a defender of the Constitution against those who would dishonor it. "I am honored that something that was indefensible was pursued and that I had the opportunity to defend the Constitution," the president said. He added that he "never" considered resigning because "I wouldn't do that to the Constitution. I wouldn't do that to the presidency. I wouldn't do that to the history of this country." This revisionism is extraordinary in its brazenness.

There are countless moments that demonstrate Bill Clinton's relentless duplicity—for example, when he looked up at the first lady during his 1999 State of the Union address, and said to a national television audience, "I honor her" and mouthed to her the words "I love you"—even as he is chronically unfaithful to her. Or when Mr. Clinton told a frustrated Ms. Lewinsky that he "might be alone" and available in a few years in response to a threat that she might tell her parents about the relationship. Or when he gave Lewinsky a copy of Walt Whitman's *Leaves of Grass* ("the most sentimental gift he had given me . . . it's beautiful and it meant a lot to me"), which also happens to be the book he gave to Hillary Rodham while they were dating. Or when he explained to an aide that his relationship with Ms. Lewinsky was based on altruism and the fact that he "felt a need to help troubled people, and it was hard for him to cut himself off from doing that." Or when the president told the grand jury that his sexual relationship with Ms. Lewinsky didn't begin until 1996, even though Ms. Lewinsky testified that it began on November 15, 1995—testimony corroborated by statements she made to her friends at the time (White House records also show that Ms. Lewinsky departed the White House at 12:18 A.M. the morning of November 16). The reason the president lied about the date the affair began is because in 1996 Ms. Lewinsky was a full-time employee but in 1995 she was an intern—and, according to her testimony, during their first sexual encounter the president tugged at her intern pass and said that "this" may be a problem.

We have witnessed those celebrated Clinton lies that pose as clever semantic tricks—for example, when asked during his grand jury testimony whether he dissembled during his civil deposition when he said, "I was never alone with her [Lewinsky]," the president answered, "it depends on how you define *alone*." Or the president's response to a statement made during the Jones deposition, when his lawyer told Judge Wright "there is absolutely no sex of any kind in any manner, shape or form" that occurred between Mr. Clinton and Ms. Lewinsky. The president later defended the truthfulness of this statement by telling the grand jury, "It depends on what the meaning of the word *is* is." But in a letter to Judge Wright, the president's lawyer admitted that he unknowingly vouched for a lie when he made the statement he did.

Bill Clinton has disgraced the American presidency. And he is a man without shame or self-awareness; at times he speaks as if he were living in a make-believe world. Consider Mr. Clinton's explanation for refusing to say more about the specifics of his relationship with Ms. Lewinsky, even though it went to the heart of the criminal case against him; it was, he said, "an effort to preserve the dignity of the office I hold."

Two days before the Senate voted to acquit the president I wrote in an opinion editorial that the Clinton Scandals (in all their sordid manifestations) will go on because with Bill Clinton there are always more shoes that will drop, more ugly facts that will come to light. Less than two weeks later the *Wall Street Journal* published an article in which an Arkansas nursing home operator, Juanita Broaddrick, made credible allegations that twenty-one years ago Bill Clinton raped and sexually assaulted her. Mrs. Broaddrick elaborated on her charge in a gripping *Dateline NBC* interview. According to Broaddrick, Mr. Clinton made a campaign stop at Broaddrick's nursing home in Van Buren, Arkansas, and invited her to visit his campaign office in Little Rock (Broaddrick was then a campaign volunteer for gubernatorial candidate Clinton). A week later she was staying at the Camelot Hotel in Little Rock and Mr. Clinton suggested they meet in the hotel coffee shop, but Mr. Clinton called later and asked her to have coffee in her room instead. They did, and after talking briefly Mr. Clinton suddenly

> *turned me around and started kissing me, and that was a real shock. I first pushed him away and just told him "no." . . . The second time he tries to kiss me he starts biting on my lip. . . . And then he forces me down on the bed. I just was very frightened, and I tried to get away from him and I told him "no." . . . He wouldn't listen to me. . . . He was such a different person at that moment, he was just a vicious, awful person.*

Juanita Broaddrick says that after being raped by Mr. Clinton, her lip swollen and bleeding, he put on his sunglasses and said, "You better get some ice on that." And then he left.

According to Mrs. Broaddrick, one reason she never reported the incident was because she didn't think anyone would believe her accusations made against a rising young politician who was the state attorney general at the time. She says she signed a false affidavit in order to avoid testimony in the Paula Jones case, but she finally came forward when she was interviewed by Judge Starr's investigators. According to her son Kevin, a lawyer, "I told my mother—and she understood it—that this was another whole level. She knew it was one thing to lie in a civil trial so she could get away from all this, but another to lie to federal prosecutors and possibly a grand jury."

Mrs. Broaddrick's charges are supported by at least five witnesses to whom she described the alleged rape within hours or days; her friend Norma Rogers-Kelsay, who accompanied Broaddrick to Little Rock on the day of the alleged incident, tells of receiving a call from an upset Broaddrick shortly after the encounter with Mr. Clinton. Rogers-Kelsay claims she rushed to Broaddrick's room, found her in tears, her mouth red and swollen, her pantyhose torn in the crotch, looking as if "she had been mugged."

The White House would not answer questions about Mr. Clinton's whereabouts on the date of the alleged rape, though Arkansas newspaper accounts indicate Bill Clinton was in Little Rock that day. In addition, there are statements by three individuals that in March 1991 then–Governor Clinton, on the verge of running for president, called Broaddrick out of a nursing home meeting to speak with her—and, according to Broaddrick, apologized to her for the attack thirteen years earlier. It is also worth noting that there does not appear to be any incentive—financial, political, or legal—for Mrs. Broaddrick to lie. The president's only response to date has been a statement by his lawyer calling Mrs. Broaddrick's charge "absolutely false. Beyond that," he said, "we are not going to comment."

This is extraordinary: Mr. Clinton is accused of having committed a terrible violent crime, but he refuses to shed *any* light on the allegation, his whereabouts at the time of the alleged incident, his relationship with Mrs. Broaddrick, or anything else. One person close to the president did tell NBC's Claire Shipman that "if there was an encounter, it may have been consensual." Not according to Mrs. Broaddrick.

There are only two possibilities: Juanita Broaddrick is either telling one of the most wicked lies ever told about an American president, or Mr. Clinton is a rapist. One would think that credible allegations of rape and sexual assault against a president would cause the national media to aggressively pursue this story and demand some answers; but much of the media, suffering from "scandal fatigue," let the story die. For obvious reasons Mr. Clinton has decided this matter is closed, but it is astonishing that so many journalists have complied. This is a story most of them not only did not want to investigate, but they did not even press the president to answer the charges in more detail—perhaps because many of them were afraid where the evidence might lead. In any event, the list of women who have accused the president of being a sexual predator continues to grow—and so, too, does the moral corruption enveloping Mr. Clinton. Bill Clinton once came across as a likable rogue, but as in Oscar Wilde's *The Picture of Dorian Gray*, the reality that is underneath is not likable; it is, in fact, extremely ugly.

That transformation is not just happening before the eyes of political conservatives. Immediately following a *Larry King Live* interview with Juanita Broaddrick's son Kevin, former Clinton aide David Gergen said, "Well, Larry, I kept thinking what mother would tell her son that she had been raped if it hadn't happened. That's what really gave me pause. I think it added to the credibility of the story. . . . [Broaddrick's son] was persuasive." And there was this admission by former Clinton White House press secretary Dee Dee Myers: "I certainly am not going to raise any questions about the credibility of Juanita Broaddrick or her son Kevin." CNN's senior political analyst Jeff Greenfield interjected at that point. "I am actually astonished almost at where the last two statements leave us," Greenfield said. "The two people who worked for the president are at least unwilling to say, 'No, I believe the president, that nothing happened that amounts to an assault.'"

Later in the program there was this extraordinary exchange:

King: Dee Dee, how do you explain—I mean, we know what womanizers are and we know there are men who like women and [there] are adulterers. But rape? I mean, you know this man. You worked with him. Rape.

Myers: I can't explain it. And again, we haven't heard anything from Bill Clinton other than the lawyers—the denials of his lawyers.

King: But the lawyers weren't there. So . . .

Myers: The lawyers weren't there. I don't know what the story is. I don't—how do I explain it to myself? I can't.

King: I think as Jeff pointed out, you should be saying, well, "No chance."

Myers: I did that for a while, Larry. I don't do that anymore.

King: David, what's your comment on that? You were there, too. You should be saying, "No chance."

Gergen: I respect Dee Dee Myers, and I—you know, she went through an awful lot. She got banged around a lot in a very tough job. And she was sent out to say things sometimes that I am sure she wondered at the time whether they were true or not. And I think a lot of people who have worked for the president unfortunately have come away feeling, well, we can't quite be sure.

This utter lack of faith in the president's word and the palpable discomfort—even shame—in having worked for him is now a common pattern among former Clinton loyalists. For example, ex–Clinton adviser George Stephanopoulos was asked if, knowing what he now knows about the president, the American people should have elected him. Stephanopoulos answered, "No. I don't think so." Asked by *Newsweek* magazine if he is proud to have worked for the president, the person who was once one of Mr. Clinton's fiercest public defenders answered, "If I knew everything then that I know now, of course I wouldn't [have worked for him]. . . . I don't think he'd be fit enough to be elected." Ms. Myers was asked by CNBC's Chris Matthews if she would have gone to work for Mr. Clinton had she known more about him. "If I had it to do over again," Myers said, "knowing what I know now, of course not." She has written that the president's relationship with Monica Lewinsky "was so reckless as to seem pathological." Mike McCurry, another former Clinton press secretary, told the BBC that the Lewinsky affair showed "incredibly bizarre personal behavior. I feel deeply disappointed, hurt, and a bit flabbergasted he could be so reckless. I have enormous doubts because of the recklessness of his behavior." And Betsey Wright, Mr. Clinton's chief of staff when he was governor and the woman in charge of handling what she called "bimbo eruptions" during the 1992 campaign, told the *Arkansas Democrat-Gazette* that "I feel personally betrayed. I feel personally lied to. I feel that he was so stupid, to be such a smart man. And I think he's got a sickness. I'm serious about that."

In the end only five House Democrats voted to impeach, and not a single Democratic senator voted to convict the president, despite the fact that they were presented with overwhelming evidence of criminal wrongdoing. Senator Robert Byrd, for example, admitted Mr. Clinton's actions rise to the level of high crimes and misdemeanors. "I have no doubt that he has given false testimony under oath," Senator Byrd said. "There are indications he did indeed obstruct justice." Yet Senator Byrd not only voted to acquit the president, he sponsored a motion to dismiss the Senate trial.

Senator Charles Schumer said, "It is clear that the president lied when he testified before the grand jury" and "the president has to be held to a higher standard and must be held accountable." But Senator Schumer voted against both impeachment (when he was in the House) and conviction (when he was in the Senate).

And Senator Daniel Patrick Moynihan answered "yes" when asked if (a) perjury in a civil case by the chief executive officer of the United States is an impeachable offense, (b) perjury before a grand jury is an impeachable offense, and (c) making false and misleading statements intended to deceive the American people is an impeachable offense. But even Senator Moynihan, who surely knows better, voted against conviction.

On and on it went, with Democrat after Democrat calling the president's conduct "reprehensible," "immoral," "indefensible," "unforgivable," and "unacceptable," yet all the while building a frantic defense of the proposition that a president who commits multiple felony crimes should remain in office.

No one can seriously argue that perjury and obstruction of justice aren't high crimes and misdemeanors—least of all members of the United States Senate. After all, it was lying before a federal grand jury that convinced an overwhelming number of senators on both sides of the aisle to remove Judge Walter L. Nixon Jr. in 1989. Here is what Senator Herb Kohl said at that time, in words that typified the sentiments of almost all Democrats: "Judge Nixon lied to a grand jury. He misled the grand jury. These acts are indisputably criminal and warrant impeachment." Are we to believe that a president should be held to a *lower* standard than a judge?

But for the sake of the argument assume that the president's criminal conduct does not rise to the level of high crimes and misdemeanors. There was another option open to all those Democrats who claim to have been so deeply offended by what the president did. They could have called on him to resign.

If Democrats believed that what the president did was as bad as they claim, then why didn't a *single* Democratic party leader (let alone a contingent of Democrats) go to Mr. Clinton and tell him: "Mr. President, you have disgraced the office and our party. You have forfeited the moral authority necessary to lead this great party. We cannot countenance your actions and we will not allow you to be our standard-bearer. You must resign." With the honorable exception of former Representative Paul McHale, not one Democratic officeholder called on the president to resign. They were unwilling to speak truth to power.

In an attempt to convince the public that they think what the president did was *really* wrong, Democrats offered a censure resolution condemning the president for his "reprehensible" conduct with a subordinate, making false statements, delaying the discovery of truth, and dishonoring the office of president. But merely scolding the president for his acts of lawlessness was a cynical (and ultimately unsuccessful) ploy. And we now have a right to draw reasonable conclusions based on the Democratic party's failure of will and conscience. This past year's long train of events demonstrates that the Democrats are willing to hold as acceptable a standard of presidential conduct that includes sex with young interns; emphatic and repeated lies to the American people; lies to the cabinet and personal staff; lies that were then promulgated on national television, in print, and before a federal grand jury; "wars" against officers of the court; vicious lies about people he considers to be a political threat; lies during civil depositions; lies before federal grand juries; and obstruction of justice. Perhaps the best insight into the modern Democratic party was House Democrats holding a pep rally at the White House hours after the president had been impeached. Standing and cheering their man, they joined their corruption to his.

This pervasive, corrupting influence on others is a Clinton hallmark; it has manifest itself in countless ways. Consider some examples:

- Steve Grossman, national chairman of the Democratic party, who in September 1998 told Bill Clinton, "Mr. President, it seems to me that you have demonstrated, at least in my adult lifetime, a higher commitment to the kind of moral leadership that I value in public service and public policy than any person I have ever met. . . . Our prayer for you . . . is that you will continue to provide the kind of moral leadership to this country that has enriched the life of virtually every citizen."

- Vice President Al Gore, who gave aid, comfort, and cover to the president throughout the scandal and who proudly introduced the president on the South Lawn of the White House the day after he was impeached, calling Mr. Clinton "one of our greatest presidents."

- The entire Clinton cabinet, all of whom were looked in the eye and lied to by the president—and many of whom were then sent out to publicly testify to the truthfulness of Mr. Clinton's claim that he did not have sexual relations with Monica Lewinsky. Eventually the truth willed out and, as a *New York Times* editorial put it, "no citizen—indeed, perhaps no member of his own family—could have grasped the completeness of President Clinton's mendacity or the magnitude of his recklessness." Yet not a single cabinet member or White House aide resigned in protest.

- Senator Frank Lautenberg, who praised Larry Flynt, the pornographer who threatened to reveal in *Hustler* magazine the sexual histories of Republicans if they voted for impeachment and conviction of the president. In lauding Flynt's efforts to sexually blackmail Republicans (Flynt took out a newspaper ad offering one million dollars for incriminating leads), Senator Lautenberg declared, "Larry Flynt says his mission is against hypocrisy, and boy, I think that's a pretty good mission."

- Abbe Lowell, the chief investigative counsel for the Democrats, who argued against impeachment by dismissing the issues of lying under oath and obstruction of justice as suitable for "classroom debate" and insisting the proper focus should not be on whether the president's "statements were or were not truthful, but what were their context, what were their impact, and what were their subject matter."

- Charles Ruff, Mr. Clinton's chief defense counsel during the impeachment hearings, making this false statement to the

United States Senate: "Let me be very clear about one proposition which has been a subtheme running through some of the comments of the [House] managers over the last many days. The White House, the president, the president's agents, the president's spokesperson, no one has ever trashed, threatened, maligned, or done anything else to Monica Lewinsky. No one."

• Representative Nancy Pelosi, who was asked about whether sexually exploiting a young female intern raised questions about Bill Clinton's treatment of women, and responded by placing all the blame on Judge Starr. "There's a point of sensitivity that women have about Kenneth Starr's attitude toward women; how he's investigating, exploiting Monica Lewinsky, how he used Linda Tripp to do that . . ." Pelosi said. "And now you see the humiliation of Betty Currie."

• White House aide Sidney Blumenthal, who held a press conference after testifying before the grand jury and complained about questions he said he was "forced to answer" by Judge Starr's prosecutors. But the transcripts show that Mr. Blumenthal was lying—which is why he was later chastised by the forewoman of the grand jury, who declared, "We are very concerned about the fact that during your last visit an inaccurate representation of the events that happened was retold on the steps of the courthouse."

Michael Kelly, a lifelong Democrat and editor of *National Journal* magazine, put it well when he wrote:

The lie at the heart of the vast and varied lie that is Bill Clinton's defense is that lying is a victimless crime—and something that properly exists as a moral concern only between the liar and his maker and a few people immediately affected. But this is not so. Lying corrupts, and an absolute liar corrupts absolutely, and the corruption spread by the lies of the absolutely mendacious Clinton is becoming frightening to behold.

The Clinton-Lewinsky scandal also revealed something important about the moral sentiments of many Americans. It is said by some that the country was deeply troubled by the president's conduct but simply made a sober judgment against impeachment and conviction. In fact, a comprehensive poll conducted by the Pew Research Center for the People and the Press found that half of all Americans felt the Clinton-Lewinsky scandal was of "little or no importance."

The hard truth is that many Americans not only did not react with outrage against Mr. Clinton, they embraced him. The president attained higher approval ratings and was more admired *after* the scandal than he was before. He achieved the highest public approval rating ever recorded for a second-term president, even though according to one poll 84 percent of the public believed the president committed perjury and obstructed justice. In one recent public opinion survey, Mr. Clinton ranked first among the men Americans most admired in the world, easily outdistancing the second-place finisher, Pope John Paul II. There is another, related poll number worth noting: earlier this year a *Washington Post* poll found four in ten Americans approved of what *Hustler* magazine's Larry Flynt did—making his cash-for-sex-secrets operation more popular than Independent Counsel Starr's court-approved investigation.

To appreciate just how wide and deep the Clinton corruption has spread, consider this thought experiment: assume that in, say, 1990, a person came to you and laid out the following scenario: the president of the United States will have a squalid sexual relationship with a young intern. The president will repeatedly lie to the American people; send out his cabinet members and aides to perpetrate his lies; impede the investigation of an independent counsel; spread false and malicious rumors about those he perceives to be a threat; make unprecedented use of private investigators to discredit his critics; and be found in contempt of court. Assume that all of these things will be established as *fact*. Assume, too, that the majority of the public will be persuaded by overwhelming evidence that the president is a sexual predator, committed perjury in a civil lawsuit, lied during his testimony before a federal grand jury, and obstructed justice. Members of the president's own party will admit as much, and they will describe his actions as "immoral," "disgraceful," "reprehensible," "indefensible," "disgusting," "deceitful," and "unforgivable." More than 150 newspapers will call for his resignation. Given all of this—and even more—you are then told that the president will not only survive this scandal but his approval rating will be higher, his influence greater, his party stronger. If told this a few years ago any sensible person would have dismissed this scenario as fantastic, unfathomable, impossible. But that is exactly what has happened.

At every critical juncture during this scandal, when it seemed as if some damaging new revelation would lead to the downfall of the president, it was public opinion that rescued him. The president certainly understands this; at a March 1999 fund-raising event Mr. Clinton told the music group The Drifters, "When you were up there singing 'Stand by Me' tonight . . . I thought about how the American people have stood by me through thick and thin." And so they did.

This death of outrage is deeply disappointing. It cannot be a healthy sign when the majority of the public, confronted with overwhelming evidence of presidential wrongdoing and squalor, perjury, and obstruction of justice, rally to his side. When they think Mr. Clinton's character is bad but act as if it doesn't matter. When they hold a president to a lower standard of behavior than they say they hold people in virtually any other profession. When they are indifferent to perpetual mendacity. When they refuse to hold a president accountable for lawlessness. Or when Mr. Clinton is in many ways, for many people, the representative man of our time.

The effects of this scandal will be far-reaching. We have set some bad precedents, and taught many wrong lessons, on law, truth, public morality, fidelity, and political ethics. The majority of the American public accepted in their president—and in accepting, validated—some pernicious arguments, sordid acts, cynical lies, and criminal conduct. In ways we cannot now fully anticipate, we will pay a price for the deal that we made with William Jefferson Clinton.

Perhaps the best we can hope for is that remorse and regret set in among the public, and even among Clinton apologists. Perhaps doubts that were suppressed during the impeachment battle will emerge. Perhaps, as one liberal writer favorably disposed to the president put it, Clinton defenders—left alone with their consciences—will be forced to confront the truly bad things this president has done, feeling queasy and uneasy about the man they rallied to defend and fought so hard to keep in office. Maybe we are in for a season of second thoughts.

I hope we are. If this does happen, it will be a good thing—one of the very few good things to emerge from Bill Clinton's Year of Lies.

Appendix

The Nixon and Clinton

Administration Scandals:

A Comparison

"12 weeks and 2 million words" vs. "4 years and $40 million"

Nixon Defense: "After 12 weeks and 2 million words of televised testimony, we have reached a point at which a continued, backward-looking obsession with Watergate is causing this nation to neglect matters of far greater importance to all of the American people." (Richard Nixon, August 15, 1973)

Clinton Defense: "People here are not interested in the scandal a day in Washington. They want to know about health care, education, child care. . . . I just think that after four years and $40 million, we've got to start asking some questions about how this law is working. I think, maybe, it's not working at all well, and we ought to change the law, limit an independent counsel to one particular fact situation, get it done in a meaningful time, and let's move on." (Richard Gephardt, House Minority Leader, February 1, 1998)

A Legal Proceeding

Nixon Defense: "The time has come to turn Watergate over to the courts, where the questions of guilt or innocence belong. The time has come for the rest of us to get on with the urgent business of our nation." (Richard Nixon, August 15, 1973)

Clinton Defense: "[T]his investigation is going on, and you know what the rules for it are, and I just think as long as it's going on, I should not comment on the specific question because there's one—then there's another, then there's another. It's better to let the investigation go on and have me do my job and focus on my public responsibilities, and let this thing play out its course. That's what I think I should do, and that's what I intend to do." (Bill Clinton, February 6, 1998)

Unable to Comment on Matters Under Investigation

Nixon Defense: "As far as the matter now is concerned, it is under investigation, as it should be, by the proper legal authorities. . . . I will not comment on these matters, particularly since possible criminal charges are involved." (Richard Nixon, June 22, 1972)

Clinton Defense: "Well, I am honoring the rules of the [Starr] investigation. And if someone else is leaking unlawfully out of the grand jury proceeding, that is a different story. I am going to do—I have told the American people what I think is essential for them to know about this and what I believe they want to know. What I'm doing is going on with my work and cooperating with the investigation. And I do not believe I should answer specific questions. I don't think that's the right thing to do right now." (Bill Clinton, February 6, 1998)

On Cooperation with Investigations

Nixon Defense: "I am very proud of the fact that in this Administration we have been more forthcoming in terms of the relationship between the executive, the White House, and Congress, than any Administration in my memory. . . . I am very proud of the fact that we are forthcoming. . . . We will cooperate; we will cooperate fully with the Senate, just as we did with the grand jury, as we did with the F.B.I., and as we did with the courts when they were conducting their investigations previously in what was called the Watergate matter." (Richard Nixon, March 15, 1973)

Clinton Defense: "From the outset, the White House has taken expansive measures to cooperate fully with the OIC's [Office of the Independent Counsel] investigation. The White House promptly searched the entire Executive Office of the President for documents responsive to the OIC's subpoenas, and has produced all responsive materials." (W. Neil Eggleston and Timothy K. Armstrong, attorneys for the White House, March 17, 1998)

Promises, Promises, Promises

Nixon Defense: "I personally ordered those conducting the investigations to get all the facts and to report them directly to me right here in this office. I again ordered that all persons in the Government or at the re-election committee should cooperate fully with the F.B.I., the prosecutors, and the grand jury. I also ordered that anyone who refused to cooperate in telling the truth would be asked to resign from government service. . . . I directed that members of the White House staff should appear and testify voluntarily under oath before the Senate committee which was investigating Watergate. I was determined that we should get to the bottom of the matter, and that the truth should be fully brought out no matter who was involved." (Richard Nixon, April 30, 1973)

Clinton Defense: "Now there are a lot of other questions that are, I think, very legitimate. You have a right to ask them. You and the American people have a right to get answers. We are working very hard to comply, get all the requests for information up here. And we will give you as many answers as we can, as soon as we can, at the appropriate time, consistent with our obligation to also cooperate with the investigations. And that's not a dodge; that's really what I've— what I've—talked [about] with our people. I want to do that. I'd like for you to have more rather than less, sooner rather than later. So we will work through it as quickly as we can and get all those questions out there to you." (Bill Clinton, January 22, 1998)

Trial by Leaks

Nixon Defense: "For months, we've been at the mercy of the Judiciary Committee, [Leon] Jaworski, and the Senate Watergate Committee. They have selectively leaked material to put the President in a bad light . . . you are in a position where these three units are out to screw you to the wall. How do you combat this when they are out to get your ass?" (Ken Clawson, deputy director of White House communications, May 26, 1974)

Clinton Defense: "Mr. Starr leaks everything that goes to the grand jury. Those thugs are getting in, ask people in the White House about campaign strategy, legislative strategy, and they'll be on the phone to Jesse Helms, who Mr. Starr owes his appointment to, so fast your head would swim. If there's something that they want to know, if they want to know about somebody spreading rumors, all they got to do is call me before the grand jury. And I think that what we have here is a relationship where we have a known pattern of leaks, which is criminal behavior from Mr. Starr and the people that work for him." (James Carville, chief strategist for Clinton's 1992 presidential campaign, February 26, 1998)

Leaks Aimed to Hurt the President

Nixon Defense: "This information, which has been provided to *The New York Times* either by a member of the House Judiciary Committee or one of its staff members, is clearly intended to prejudice public opinion, which does not have access to the full record of the secret executive session hearings. I repeat again that this type of piecemeal revelation of executive session hearings and materials before them is a violation of due process and an absolute violation of the committee rules. In my view, if this type of process continues, where information is leaked to create a negative inference against the President, the Speaker of the House and other members of the Congress should demand an explanation from the House Judiciary Committee as to why committee rules are being so blatantly violated." (Ron Ziegler, press secretary, May 25, 1974)

Clinton Defense: "This is information, testimony, that's before a grand jury. And in our system, testimony for a grand jury has to be kept secret. In fact, if you violate that secrecy, it's a violation of federal law. And I find it extraordinarily troubling, one more day, to find one more leak from someone with a political ax to grind, leaking information from the grand jury in violation of the law. . . . Let's find out who's behind these criminal leaks, and let's get to the bottom of that. Because someone wishes the President ill, and they are lying and leaking every day." (Paul Begala, counselor to the president, February 6, 1998)

On Executive Privilege

Nixon Defense: "[T]he confidentiality of the office of the President would always be suspect. Persons talking with a President would never again be sure that recordings or notes of what they said would not at some future time be made public, and they would guard their words against that possibility. . . . I shall therefore vigorously oppose any actions which would set a precedent that would cripple all future Presidents by inhibiting conversations between them and the persons they look to for advice." (Richard Nixon, August 15, 1973)

Clinton Defense: "The President of the United States, if he is to perform his constitutionally assigned duties, must be able to obtain the most candid, forthright, and well-informed advice from his advisors. . . . [W]e have also made clear our firm conviction that the OIC can have no legitimate interest in the White House staff's discussions of political or legal strategy. . . . [T]he White House has reserved the invocation of executive privilege to that inner core of conversations that cannot be disclosed without materially harming the ability of future Presidents to confer with advisors candidly." (W. Neil Eggleston and Timothy K. Armstrong, March 17, 1998)

Waiving Executive Privilege

Nixon Defense: "[T]his administration has, I think, gone further in terms of waiving executive privilege than any Administration in my memory." (Richard Nixon, August 22, 1973)

Clinton Defense: [Responding to a question on invoking executive privilege] "It is hard for me to imagine a circumstance in which that would be an appropriate thing for me to do." (Bill Clinton, March 8, 1994)

On the Necessity of Executive Privilege

Nixon Defense: "It is absolutely necessary, if the President is to be able to do his job as the country expects, that he be able to talk openly and candidly with his advisers about issues and individuals. This kind of frank discussion is only possible when those who take part in it know that what they say is in strictest confidence. . . . It is even more important that the confidentiality of conversations between a President and his advisers be protected. This is no mere luxury, to be dispensed with whenever a particular issue raises sufficient uproar. It is absolutely essential to the conduct of the Presidency, in this and in all future Administrations." (Richard Nixon, August 15, 1973)

Clinton Defense: "In this context [counsel to the president], the presidential communications and attorney-client privilege are mutually self-reinforcing. Both exist to guarantee that the President receives necessary advice and input with the candor that can be secured only when advisors are free from apprehension about how third parties or the public may view them. When government attorneys or other advisors doubt the confidentiality of their communications, they will of necessity speak guardedly, hedging their recommendations with a view toward preserving the natural human desire to be well thought of by others. Such caution extracts a heavy toll, for it prevents the President from receiving the candid assistance necessary to run the government effectively and thereby serve the national interest." (W. Neil Eggleston and Timothy K. Armstrong, March 17, 1998)

On Executive Privilege and Nonofficial Business

Nixon Defense: "The argument is often raised that these tapes are somehow different because the conversations may bear on illegal acts, and because the commission of illegal acts is not an official duty. This misses the point entirely. Even if others, from their own standpoint, may have been thinking about how to cover up an illegal act, from my standpoint, I was thinking about how to uncover the illegal acts. . . . [T]he precedent would not be one concerning illegal actions only; it would be one that would risk exposing private Presidential conversations involving the whole range of official duties." (Richard Nixon, August 15, 1973)

Clinton Defense: "With respect to the Lewinsky matter, the grand jury is inquiring into actions allegedly taken by the President while in office—indeed, actions that allegedly occurred in the White House itself. And as to the President's deposition, the mere fact that the [Paula] Jones case involves alleged conduct before the President took office does not mean that the advice he is given concerning his constitutional duties somehow becomes 'private.' . . . Any advice sought by the President to deal with the threat of impeachment is, by its very nature, official—not private." (W. Neil Eggleston and Timothy K. Armstrong, March 17, 1998)

Court Ruling on Executive Privilege

Nixon Case: "[T]he allowance of the privilege to withhold evidence that is demonstrably relevant in a criminal trial would cut deeply into the guarantee of due process of law and gravely impair the basic function of the courts. A President's acknowledged need for confidentiality in the communications of his office is general in nature, whereas the constitutional need for production of relevant evidence in a criminal proceeding is specific and central to the fair adjudication of a particular criminal case in the administration of justice." (Chief Justice Warren Burger, 1974)

Clinton Case: "The court finds that the categories of testimony sought by the OIC from [Bruce] Lindsey and [Sidney] Blumenthal are all likely to contain relevant evidence that is important to the grand jury's investigation. . . . The testimony sought and withheld based on executive privilege is likely to shed light on that inquiry, whether exculpatory or inculpatory. . . . If there were instructions from the President to obstruct justice or efforts to suborn perjury, such actions likely took the form of conversations involving the President's closest advisors, including Lindsey and Blumenthal. . . . [This evidence] would constitute some of the most relevant and important evidence to the grand jury investigation." (Judge Norma Holloway Johnson, 1998)

On Ignorance of Wrongdoing

Nixon Defense: "It is clear that unethical, as well as illegal, activities took place in the course of that campaign. None of these took place with my specific approval or knowledge." (Richard Nixon, May 22, 1973)

Clinton Defense: "That was the other campaign [referring to the Democratic National Committee, not the Clinton-Gore campaign] that had problems with that, not mine." (Bill Clinton, November 8, 1996)

On Political Opponents

Nixon Defense: "If you share my beliefs in these goals—if you want the mandate you gave this Administration to be carried out—

then I ask for your help to insure that those who would exploit Watergate in order to keep us from doing what we were elected to do will not succeed." (Richard Nixon, August 15, 1973)

Clinton Defense: "And it's obvious, I think, to the American people that this has been a hard, well-financed, vigorous effort over a long period of time by people who could not contest the ideas that I brought to the table . . . and certainly can't quarrel with the consequences and the results of my service. And, therefore, personal attack seems legitimate." (Bill Clinton, April 30, 1998)

On Political Opponents Seeking to Undo the Election

Nixon Defense: "I would think that some political figures, some members of the press perhaps, some members of the television, perhaps, would exploit it [Watergate]. . . . There are a great number of people in this country that would prefer that I do resign. There are a great number of people in this country that didn't accept the mandate of 1972. . . . But what I am saying is this. People who did not accept the mandate of '72, who do not want the strong America that I want to build, who do not want the foreign policy leadership that I want to give, that do not want to cut down the size of this Government bureaucracy that burdens us so greatly and to give more of our Government back to the people, people who do not want these things naturally would exploit any issues. If it weren't Watergate, anything else in order to keep the President from doing his job. . . . On the other hand, I'm not going to fail. I'm here to do a job, and I'm going to do the best I can." (Richard Nixon, August 22, 1973)

Clinton Defense: "We get a politically motivated prosecutor who is allied with the right-wing opponents of my husband, who has literally spent four years . . . doing everything possible to try to make some accusation against my husband. . . . This is the great story here for anybody willing to find it and write about it and explain it, is this vast right-wing conspiracy that has been conspiring against my husband since the day he announced for president." (Hillary Rodham Clinton, January 27, 1998)

On Being Persecuted

Nixon Defense: "Nixon and I discussed that—that the office [of the special prosecutor] would continue [after the firing of Archibald Cox]; his only words on it were: 'I want a prosecution, not a persecution.'" (Robert Bork, solicitor general under President Nixon, quoted in *Nixon: An Oral History of His Presidency*, by Gerald S. Strober and Deborah Hart Strober, 1994)

Clinton Defense: "I think the office of the independent counsel has made him [Starr] nutty and I don't understand it. This kind of fishing expedition makes him not a Whitewater special prosecutor, but a general persecutor of the president." (Cass Sunstein, former Justice Department adviser, January 22, 1998)

Partisan Prosecutors

Nixon Defense: "Archibald Cox . . . was also one of the most articulate spokesmen for the liberal wing of the Democratic Party. He had been very much involved in Jack Kennedy's campaign in 1960— that is not the characteristic of an impartial special prosecutor." (Richard Kleindienst, attorney general, quoted in *Nixon: An Oral History of His Presidency*, by Gerald S. Strober and Deborah Hart Strober, 1994)

Clinton Defense: "I think Mr. Starr was a political person who was put there by a political judge, as a result of political pressure from political senators." (James Carville, February 24, 1998)

Prosecution by the Opposition

Nixon Defense: "Archibald Cox and the people who served with him were operating in an extreme way in the use of power. . . . Cox deserved to be fired. That doesn't mean the cover-up should have succeeded; it simply means that Archibald Cox should have been fired because he was a partisan extremist in the pursuit of Richard Nixon. He was not conducting a balanced inquiry into the presidency of the United States." (Ron Ziegler, quoted in *Nixon: An Oral History of His Presidency*, by Gerald S. Strober and Deborah Hart Strober, 1994)

Clinton Defense: "He's [Ken Starr] after the President. . . . We have many indications that Mr. Starr has political roots in the conservative movements of this country. He volunteered to file a brief on behalf of Paula Jones. We certainly know that he has a political agenda, and in this case, Cokie [Roberts], it really does seem to me that an affidavit in the middle of a civil case in which the case itself was thrown out and the testimony of Ms. Lewinsky was found to be inadmissible—we're talking about a criminal indictment of a young woman. . . . And we're talking about a criminal process that goes back over five years, that started out investigating the President. What has happened to this independent counsel?" (Lanny Davis, former White House counsel, May 3, 1998)

On the History of Prosecutors

Nixon Defense: "Cox will be a disaster. He has been fanatically anti-Nixon all the years I've known him." (Henry Kissinger, secretary of state, quoted in *Kennedy & Nixon,* by Christopher Matthews, 1996)

Clinton Defense: "[Ken Starr] was a right-wing partisan, who was put in by a right-wing partisan. And he will conduct a partisan investigation." (James Carville, February 23, 1998)

On Biased Vendettas

Nixon Defense: "If [Elliot] Richardson [Nixon's nominee for attorney general who was forced to select a special prosecutor in order to be confirmed by the Senate] had searched specifically for the man whom I would have least trusted to conduct so politically sensitive an investigation in an unbiased way, he could hardly have done better than choose Archibald Cox." (Richard Nixon, quoted in *Kennedy & Nixon,* by Christopher Matthews, 1996)

Clinton Defense: "Look, [Ken Starr] is on a vendetta. He's obsessed with getting Bill Clinton. He spent $40 million to try to get him. . . . $40 million to do what? To try to get this man. And you know what it ends up with? Sex." (James Carville, February 26, 1998)

"Get on with the Job" vs. "The Business of the People"

Nixon Defense: "These are matters that cannot wait. They cry out for action now. And either we, your elected representatives here in Washington, ought to get on with the jobs that need to be done—for you—or every one of you ought to be demanding to know why." (Richard Nixon, August 15, 1973)

Clinton Defense: "The most important thing is that I can go back now and continue the work that I'm doing. That's the most important thing to me. I want to get back to the business of the people." (Bill Clinton, April 2, 1998)

Distractions from Vital Work

Nixon Defense: "It is also essential that we not be so distracted by events such as this [Watergate] that we neglect the vital work before us, before this nation, before America, at a time of critical importance to America and to the world." (Richard Nixon, April 30, 1973)

Clinton Defense: "[I]n all of my travels I have not heard anybody in America say we'd like to hear more about this. What they say is, we'd like to hear what you're going to do about tobacco, about Social Security, about balancing the budget, about fixing education, about expanding Medicare, and a patients' bill of rights, those are the things that we're working on here at the White House." (Paul Begala, April 7, 1998)

On Completing the People's Mandate

Nixon Defense: "Last November, the American people were given the clearest choice of this century. Your votes were a mandate, which I accepted, to complete the initiatives we began in my first term and to fulfill the promises I made for my second term." (Richard Nixon, August 15, 1973)

Clinton Defense: "I was elected to do a job. I think the American people . . . know I have worked very, very hard for them. And I think they know now, more often than not, the ideas I had and the things I fought for turned out to be right in terms of the consequences for the American people. I think they know all that. And I'm just going to keep showing up for work. I'm going to do what I was hired to do. And I'm going to try to keep getting good results for them." (Bill Clinton, February 6, 1998)

Successes Threatened by Investigation

Nixon Defense: "This Administration was elected to control inflation, to reduce the power and size of Government, to cut the cost of Government so that you can cut the cost of living, to preserve and defend those fundamental values that have made America great, to keep the nation's military strength second to none. . . . These are great goals. They are worthy of a great people. And I would not be true to your trust if I let myself be turned aside from achieving those goals." (Richard Nixon, August 15, 1973)

Clinton Defense: "[T]he budget bill . . . worked, that we have surplus, that we have an untold number of new jobs. The president's policies worked; the American people agree. . . . [T]hat's the reason the American people don't want him mired in these details, don't want him part of the media frenzy. They want him doing the nation's business because his policies work." (Lanny Davis, February 6, 1998)

Focus on the Future

Nixon Defense: "We must not stay so mired in Watergate that we fail to respond to challenges of surpassing importance to America and the world. We cannot let an obsession with the past destroy our hopes for the future." (Richard Nixon, August 15, 1973)

Clinton Defense: "[W]hat I would say to you is that what is essential is that we [Bill Clinton and I] focus on the issues that we were elected to focus upon. And in the discussions that we have had over this past two days, we've been focusing on issues like Iraq, where we are considering if diplomatic solutions fail taking military action. We've been focusing on the peace process in Northern Ireland that gives the chance for the first time in generations, after centuries of conflict, for people to find a way through. We've been focusing on the problems of the world economy, that if they're not tackled could have a serious impact on the living standards of people here and people in Britain, as well as people out in Asia. These are the important questions for me: schools, hospitals, crime, living standards, jobs that people want us to focus upon. And I believe that it is absolutely essential that we stay focused upon those things, and that we deliver for our people what we were elected to deliver." (Tony Blair, British prime minister, February 6, 1998)

Legislation Suffers

Nixon Defense: "Legislation vital to your health and well-being sits unattended on the Congressional calendar. Confidence at home and abroad in our economy, our currency and our foreign policy is being sapped by uncertainty. Critical negotiations are taking place on strategic weapons, on troop levels in Europe that can affect the security of this nation and the peace of the world long after Watergate is forgotten." (Richard Nixon, August 15, 1973)

Clinton Defense: "But the time that this [Ken Starr's investigation] has taken, I think, is becoming unreasonable because it does take the attention of the country away from the things that we most should be working on—education, health care, pensions, jobs, wages, the economy, moving the country in the right direction." (Richard Gephardt, May 1, 1998)

On Media Fixations with Scandal

Nixon Defense: "We must move on from Watergate to the business of the people—the business of the people is continuing with initiatives we began in the first Administration. . . . We've had 30 minutes of this press conference. I have yet to have, for example, one question on the business of the people." (Richard Nixon, August 22, 1973)

Clinton Defense: "I'm standing here on a day that we need to focus—and this is literally part of what the whole question of executive privilege was about . . . I have to take the time on a day that we are focusing on a very real question of the balance of forces on the Indian subcontinent, a matter in which the United States has a keen and real interest. We are distracted in this very room at this very moment by this [the Lewinsky] matter." (Mike McCurry, White House press secretary, May 28, 1998)

Media Millionaires and Americans

Nixon Defense: "If [Ben] Bradlee [the executive editor of the *Washington Post* during Watergate] ever left the Georgetown cocktail circuit, where he and his pals dine on third-hand information and

gossip and rumor, he might discover out here the real America."
(Charles Colson, special counsel to President Nixon, quoted in
Kennedy & Nixon, by Christopher Matthews, 1996)

Clinton Defense: "What media millionaires do share is a lack of
interest in discussing this sort of subject [raising the minimum wage]
on TV, which is why it rarely comes up. An examination of substantive issues doesn't compete with sex, lies, and audio tapes. . . . But
theirs is not the agenda of the public, which clearly has rejected sex
for substance." (Robert Scheer, *Los Angeles Times* columnist, February 17, 1998)

On Distractions in Office

Nixon Defense: "It is imperative that the work of the Office of
the President not be impeded and your staff must be in a position to
focus their attention on the vital areas of domestic and international
concerns that face you, rather than being diverted by the daily rumors
and developments in the Watergate case." (H.R. Haldeman, assistant
to the president, April 29, 1973)

Clinton Defense: "The Lewinsky investigation . . . is inextricably intertwined with the daily presidential agenda, and thus has a
substantial impact on the president's ability to discharge his obligations. . . . The president's ability to work with Congress to enact legislation is likewise affected by the Lewinsky investigation. Certain
legislators have been described as 'throwing up their hands at the
prospect of doing any serious business,' thereby significantly affect-
ing the president's domestic agenda. . . . I understand that the Lewinsky investigation also affected the president's ability to address
foreign policy matters." (Charles Ruff, White House counsel, May 27,
1998)

Denials—Believe It or Not

Nixon Defense: "I stated in very specific terms—and I state
again to every one of you listening tonight—these facts: I had no prior
knowledge of the Watergate break-in; I neither took part in nor knew
about any of the subsequent cover-up activities; I neither authorized
nor encouraged subordinates to engage in illegal or improper campaign tactics." (Richard Nixon, August 15, 1973)

Clinton Defense: "Let me say, first of all, I want to reiterate what I said yesterday. The allegations are false, and I would never ask anybody to do anything other than tell the truth. Let's get to the big issues there—about the nature of the relationship and whether I suggested anybody not to tell the truth. That is false." (Bill Clinton, January 22, 1998)

Denials on Tape

Nixon Defense: "Perjury is an awful hard rap to prove. . . . Be damned sure you say, 'I don't remember . . . I can't recall.'" (Richard Nixon, Oval Office tapes, March 21, 1973)

Clinton Defense: [Taped conversation with Gennifer Flowers, regarding how she obtained her state job] "I never thought about that. . . . If they ever ask if you've talked to me about it, you can say no." (Bill Clinton, 1992) [When Ms. Flowers told him she lied under oath to a grievance committee, the then-governor said on tape, "Good for you."]

On Whether the President Might Resign

Nixon Defense: "The answer . . . is no." (Richard Nixon, August 22, 1973)

Clinton Defense: "Never." (Bill Clinton, February 6, 1998)

On Criminality of the President

Nixon: "I am not a crook." (Richard Nixon, November 17, 1973)

Clinton: "[President Clinton] is a man who I do not think is a crook." (James Carville, February 24, 1998)

And Yet . . .

"The idea that Ken Starr's little nickel-dime sex investigation here is somehow or another akin to Watergate is the most ludicrous thing I've ever heard." (James Carville, May 8, 1998)